CONCILIUM

THEOLOGY IN THE AGE OF RENEWAL

CONCILIUM

CONCILIUM/VOL. 48

CANON LAW

THE FUTURE OF CANON LAW

edited by ✠ NEOPHYTOS EDELBY
TEODORO JIMÉNEZ-URRESTI
PETRUS HUIZING, S.J.

VOLUME 48

CONCILIUM
theology in the age of renewal

PAULIST PRESS
NEW YORK, N.Y./PARAMUS, N.J.

PAULIST PRESS
EXECUTIVE OFFICES: 304 W. 58th Street, New York, N.Y. and 404 Sette Drive, Paramus, N.J.
Publisher: John A. Carr, C.S.P.

EDITORIAL OFFICES: 304 W. 58th Street, New York, N.Y.
Executive Editor: Kevin A. Lynch, C.S.P.
Managing Editor: Urban P. Intondi

Printed and bound in the United States of America by Wickersham Printing Co., Lancaster, Pa.

CONTENTS

vii

PART II

BIBLIOGRAPHICAL SURVEY

PART III

DOCUMENTATION CONCILIUM
Office of the Executive Secretary
Nijmegen, Netherlands

PREFACE

✠ Néophytos Edelby/*Alep, Syria*
Teodoro Jiménez-Urresti/*Madrid, Spain*
Petrus Huizing, S.J./*Nijmegen, Netherlands*

The Church is human as well as divine. She is "a social reality in history" (CMW 44) which "while transcending all limits of time and of race . . . is destined to extend to all regions of the earth and so to enter into the history of mankind" (C 9). She is divine because the Holy Spirit "vivifies ecclesiastical institutions as a kind of soul" (CMA 4), and human and historical because "the pilgrim Church in her sacraments and institutions which pertain to this present time takes on the appearance of this passing world" (C 48).

The dynamism of the Spirit therefore makes itself present with a signified and active presence of saving life in the historical dynamism of the sacraments and institutions of the Church. Thus the sacramentary character of the Church is not static; rather, the Church as "a universal sacrament of salvation", as *"sacramentum mundi"*, carries in herself the vital dynamism proper to the Spirit at the pace of, in the middle of, and even incorporating, the dynamism of the world itself—"of this passing world".

Through being historical although divine at the same time, the Church cannot be brought into being at one particular moment, but "gradually progresses in her activity to carry out God's design" (CMA 6). But she does not walk alone in and with her

1

history, but "goes forward together with humanity and experiences the same earthly lot which the world does" (CMW 40). Because of this historicity the Church fulfills her historical mission in the history of humanity; she works out her *"historia salutis"*, which consists in making herself "the leaven of history" that must be transformed so as to place her under the aegis of Christ who is the center, the axis, the key, the goal and the Lord of human history and of the history of salvation (cf. CMW 41, 44-45).

The Church on her historical way, although "she is invigorated by the power of the risen Lord" and "is comforted by the grace of God" and so "in the weakness of the flesh does not lose her absolute reality", nevertheless "to take sinners into its bosom" "is in need of permanent reform as a human and earthly institution" (C 8-9; E 6). Furthermore, she has to overcome not only these "internal difficulties" but also "external difficulties" (C 8), since no small part of her historical effectiveness "depends on external realities" (CMW 44) which she needs to put on in order to carry out her historical mission.

On the other hand, the Church "matures her judgment" and her consciousness of herself in her history (DR 12) and so "realizes that in working out her relationship with the world she always has great need of the ripening which comes with experience of the centuries" (CMW 43). But this maturity is acquired not only from her own experience or history but also from the experience of the world in which she exists and whose sacrament of salvation she is: "She can and ought to be enriched by the development of human social life" (CMW 44); therefore she can talk to the world "in the light of the gospel and of human experience" (CMW 46), in her "pilgrim progress toward the consummation of human history" which is in reestablishing all things in Christ (cf. Eph. 1, 10, CMW 45).

These principles, formulated by Vatican Council II on the historicity and dynamism of the Church and her saving mission, can and should lead to some very important conclusions for

Canon Law, whose task is precisely to regulate this historical activity of the Church as a saving social institution (Neumann).

1. In the first place the Church, in her structures and positive canonical activities, has to keep herself in a position of the greatest possible fidelity to her vocation—that is, to the very nature of her mission and divine structures, closely observing her foundations and her theological, sacramentary objectives. We have previously examined several of the great principles which apply in this respect in the Canon Law volumes of *Concilium* published in 1965, 1967 and 1968.

But we also need to know what Protestant teaching in its various systems can tell us about these great principles (Steinmuller) and more particularly the latest developments of these positions which are closer to ours than they used to be (Dombois). Their reflections can help us in our task of "constant renewal". The pastoral suitability (Winninger) of canonical ordering itself can also tell us something about the requirements, formulation and functioning of internal Canon Law.

2. One of the internal difficulties which the Church has to overcome in her own history—and perhaps the most important of these difficulties—is her own inner tensions. Today these are particularly salient and in some ways show a very positive side. This is due as much to the influence of external historical realities as to the greater maturity that the laity have acquired by coming to a better understanding of themselves—by coming of age historically, as desired by Vatican Council II, with the consequent noble desire to remain faithful to their own particular active vocation. There are historical tensions between those who see "the (institutionalized) charism of the apostles" in the Church and the so-called "charismatics". Sometimes the latter are better, or at any rate quicker, than the former at living the life of faith more fully or in seeing the demands of faith with greater speed or clarity, and so they clamor for renewals and reforms that are slow in coming. Such tensions—legitimate while and to the extent that they are the fruit of advances or anticipa-

tions and until they have been tested by those who preside over the Church (cf. C 12)—reflect the breath of the Spirit, which blows even on Canon Law, with powerful and special dynamism. These tensions require specific attention and study (Setién). But the correct view of these tensions and a solution will only come through study not only of the charismatic structure of the Church, the sacramentary character of the hierarchy and its function, and the nature of the "hierarchical communion"—themes which have already seen amply studied in previous volumes of *Concilium*—but also from serious reflection on the position, function and canonical rights of the lay person in the Church (Lombardía), including an examination of his rights of freedom of association (Primetshofer).

3. Other tensions arise within the Church under the influence of historical cultures and external realities. The study of the history of the Church herself within the history of the world which surrounds her and in which she is immersed, a study made easy today by the greater extent of relations between the Church and the world, gives us a much better idea of the qualitative catholicity of the Church, which cannot be identified with any particular culture or civilization; it also makes us reflect more on the influence of Roman legal culture on Canon Law. It helps us to make the distinction and even the necessary separation between the cultural trappings of Canon Law and its theological entrails.

In fact it could be said that the Church considered historically, even with all her history and the trappings of 2,000 years of experience, is today passing from her infancy to her youth, since considered as a whole she is emerging from her almost unique historical experience of "incarnation" in Greco-Roman or Western culture and beginning a new universality and a new era together with the entire world. It is not therefore just a question of the Church as an historical reality being a dynamic reality in herself, nor of her also having to be dynamic in the formulation and realization of her internal discipline. Her dynamism, reflected in Canon Law as well as in other things, is also deeply influenced by the historical and cultural dynamism of the world to whose outlines she conforms. And if the Church and Canon Law were not to follow the dynamic rhythm of this history of the world, the Church's canonical clothing would become a strait-jacket tying her up in a series of details that would impede her pastoral-historical progress. Neumann gives us his views on this subject.

4. On the other hand an examination of the experience or history of the Church and her Canon Law makes us see better how the Church, being "a body of churches" (C 23) so that the one and only Catholic Church comes into being in and from the individual churches (cf. C 23) and has to respect the autonomy of each individual church and the resulting diversity of churches in the Church, should guard the riches of the diversity of patri-monies and traditions, of rights and customs, of theological, cultural and disciplinary structures of the individual churches (cf. C 13, E 5)—and this within the undivided Catholicity (C 23).

From this point of view the articles in this volume should be read in conjunction with those by Hajjar, De Vries and Edelby previously published in the 1965 and 1967 volumes. There is a need for deep, close, interecclesial and hierarchical communion around the visible head of the Church in order to avoid the risk of dispersion and the breaking up of unity; there is also a need to avoid the risk of imposing a uniformity that will hinder the development of the life of each individual church and stifle the initiative of those responsible for each church in its particular time and place. The article by Rietmeier deals with this question. Rezáč's article shows that it is even more important to avoid al-lowing one church or discipline to impose its domination on another.

5. Finally, the Church as an historical institution, if she is to establish her historical saving dialogue with the world more effectively, must "hear, distinguish and interpret the many voices of our age" in order to "understand [the constitution given to her by Christ] and adjust it more successfully to our time" (CMW 44). At each period and in every country, the Church

in her human ecclesiastical institutions—the outward expression of the divinely instituted generic, organic constitution—must, in order to carry out her historical saving—i.e., pastoral—mission, not only recognize and use theological principles but also "rely on those who live in the world, are versed in different institutions and specialities and grasp their innermost significance in the eyes of both believers and unbelievers" (CMW 44). She must also make use of "the findings of the secular sciences, especially of psychology and sociology" (CMW 62).

If any juridical ordering has a specific relationship to sociology, this is also true of Canon Law, which regulates the principles of pastoral action. Canon Law has to maintain a system of functionally adequate guidance in the social sphere to which pastoral care applies, since the Church cannot limit herself to being a simple mirror of social reality, as any ordering, including canonical, by definition tries to push society forward to new objectives (common political good, etc), to find better conditions for the well-being of her members and the common good of both society and the Church. Greely's article deals with this point.

Much more, of course, could be said about the dynamism of Canon Law. This volume of *Concilium*, which includes an article by Zužek on the Eastern Churches, limits itself to a few basic reflections and principles illustrated from historical experience. What is important is to point out the essential mobility of Canon Law within the compass of history, and as an intrinsic requirement of the historical effectiveness which the historical fulfillment of the Church's universal saving mission must have—an essential mobility based on the *essentially functional relativity* of canonical laws which has been discussed in the 1967 Canon Law volume of *Concilium* by Jiménez-Urresti.

What is often difficult is to reach the correct distinction between what every rule and canonical law has in it of historical contingency and what it enshrines as of permanent value belonging to the theological deposit laid down by Christ in the organic structure which in a general form he gave to his Church, and which is contained as a nucleus in every structural manifestation or canonical law which clads this basic nucleus. The political prudence of pastors in fidelity to the historical fulfillment of their mission and to the generic divine constitution of the Church will dictate the necessary formulation given to this contingent law. The task of the canonist is to bring his contribution to this distinction (cf. the Preface in *Concilium* 8 and the article by Jiménez-Urresti in *Concilium* 28), even though, precisely because this is moving on the very limit of what is contingent and what is permanent in order to study their limits, he may run the risk of going beyond his own limits. But he does this with the worthy object of lending his service to the hierarchy and with the effective will to be faithful to the hierarchy in full hierarchical communion, in order the better to discover the historical relativity and contingency of canonical laws so that a way may be found to the necessary mobility and necessary dynamism of Canon Law. Therefore, the canonist must give a living witness to the historicity, dynamism and pilgrim nature of the human condition in which the dynamic, divine, intra-historical mystery of the Church exists. If he does this, he can rejoice to see himself fulfilling an authentic ecclesial vocation—contributing to the historical fulfillment of the Church as sacrament.

[1] In this Preface the documents of Vatican Council II are referred to by abbreviation: C (*Constitution on the Church*); CMW (*Constitution on the Church in the Modern World*); DR (*Constitution on Divine Revelation*); CCER (*Decree on the Catholic Churches of the Eastern Rite*); CMA (*Decree on the Church's Missionary Activity*); E (*Decree on Ecumenism*).

PART I
ARTICLES

Johannes Neumann/*Tübingen, West Germany*

The Social Nature of the Church and Its Consequences for Canon Law

The Church was not "founded" like any other human society. It did not originate through free association or a social contract. The community of the Lord was "bought and paid for" by the blood of the Son of Man (1 Cor. 6, 20). The Spirit of the Lord dwells in the *ecclesia,* that band of those "called" by the Spirit before God, as in a temple (1 Cor. 3, 16; 6, 19). "Thus, the Church shines forth as 'a people made one with the unity of the Father, the Son, and the Holy Spirit.' " [1] The disciples were called by the Lord. The meaning and purpose of this choice was not an organization, but the "bearing of fruit in patience" and the following of the commandment "that you love one another" (Jn. 15, 17). Built upon the Twelve, who will judge the twelve tribes of Israel (Lk. 22, 30), the followers were to proclaim the Good News to the whole world.

While the instructions and parables of the Gospel presuppose some juridical views and institutions, it would be an exaggeration to see in these words of the Gospel final statements of "divine law" in the sense of norms that are legally sanctioned and enforcible by a human jurisdiction.[2] In general, the New Testa-

---

[1] *Constitution on the Church,* n. 4.

[2] Cf. J. Neumann, "Das 'Ius Divinum' im Kirchenrecht," in *Orientierung* 31 (1967), pp. 5-8; P. Huizing, " 'Göttliches Recht' und Kirchenverfassung," in *Stimmen der Zeit* 94 (1969), pp. 162-73.

ment thinks and speaks in cosmic rather than juridical terms. This does not prevent it from giving us an inkling of principles of Church organization.[3] When Jesus sent out his apostles for the first time (Mt. 10, 1-16), he used the institution of the *schaliach*, by which the Jews legally delegated power. As *sche-luchim* the apostles were his authoritative delegates, endowed with his authority.[4] This mandate expires when they return to Jesus.[5]

Finally, according to St. John, the risen Christ used this special delegation formula to transmit his authority to the disciples in the explicit statement, "As the Father sent me, so am I sending you" (Jn. 20, 21). The mandate he had received from the Father was thus transmitted by a formal legal gesture.

Soon Jesus' disciples adopted another institution of Judaic rabbinical legal and liturgical origin: the imposition of hands, the *semikhah*.[6] In later Judaism the teacher installed his disciple as teacher and judge by means of an imposition of hands after he had successfully finished his studies. In contrast with the *schaliach*, the *semikhah* was an unrepeatable authorization, once for all, because it not only confirmed that the disciple was able and fit to teach but also conferred divine power upon him. For the same reason it could not be made retroactive.[7]

---

[3] It must always be remembered that Jesus spoke "prophetically", not "doctrinally", and certainly not as an official "legislator". He was more concerned with conversion than with teaching. See H. Kahlefeld, *Gleichnisse und Lehrstücke im Evangelium* II (Frankfurt, 1963), p. 149.

[4] The word "apostolos" is the Greek translation of the Aramaic *schaliach*. He is the authorized representative. At the official level he has the same rights as the one who sends him. "The *schaliach* of a person is like the person himself": Strack-Billerbeck, *Kommentar zum Neuen Testament aus Talmud und Midrash* III (Munich, 1954), p. 2.

[5] Cf. E. Lohse, *Die Ordination im Spätjudentum und im Neuen Testament* (Göttingen, 1951), esp. p. 62; M. Kaiser, *Die Einheit der Kirchengewalt nach dem Zeugnis des Neuen Testamentes und der Apostolischen Väter* (Munich, 1956), p. 27; J. Neumann, *Der Spender der Firmung in der Kirche des Abendlandes bis zum Ende des kirchlichen Altertums* (Meitingen, 1963), p. 26.

[6] Cf. J. Neumann, "Salbung und Handauflegung als Heilszeichen und Rechtsakt," in *Wahrheit und Verkündigung* (Paderborn, 1957), pp. 1424-27.

[7] Cf. E. Lohse, *op. cit.*, pp. 53f.; M. Kaiser, *op. cit.*, p. 109. Whether

The writings of the New Testament show us then that the earliest Christians, pressed by definite religious or social circumstances, referred to such legal institutions and social conditions as were thought proper for the given situation. And so we find in Acts that, either because of abuses or because of a certain pluralism within the Church, a first ecclesiastical office was introduced with a definite function: the service of the "seven".[8] These "seven, filled with the Spirit and with wisdom", elected by the Hellenic section of the community, were more than just in charge of the poor and almsgiving. According to Acts they are no less than the colleagues of the Twelve for the Hellenic sector of the first community, since they were endowed with apostolic authority by virtue of the imposition of hands. This group of seven, sharing in authority, shows on the one hand their relative autonomy and, on the other, how naturally the community and their leaders seized upon and took over existing institutions, because at that time the Jewish communities of Palestine were as a rule locally administered by a college of seven, called the elders (*presbyteroi*).[9] This type of organization was taken over simply to fill a need of the community and without any particular theological consideration. The only thing one might call specifically Christian was, if one wishes to see it that way, the fact that those elected were presented to the apostles "who prayed and laid their hands on them" (Acts 6, 6).

The process was no different for the further development of offices in the organization of the community based on the prac-

the mission of Barnabas and Saul by the prophets of Antioch refers to the *semikhah* is doubtful "because those who lay on hands are not of a higher rank": cf. E. Haenchen, *Die Apostelgeschichte* (Göttingen, 121959), pp. 338 (n. 5) and 345.

[8] Cf. J. Neumann, *Der Spender der Firmung*, pp. 9-18; P. Gaechter, *Petrus und siene Zeit* (Innsbruck, 1958), p. 126; for the motivation, see H. Zimmermann, "Die Wahl der Sieben," in *Die Kirche und ihre Amter und Stände* (Cologne, 1960), pp. 364-78, esp. p. 376; P. de Vries, "Die christliche Gemeinde nach der lukanischen Theologie," in *Geist u. Leben* 41 (1968), p. 167.

[9] Flavius Josephus, *Antiquities of the Jews* IV, 8, 38; Strack-Billerbeck, *op. cit.*, II, p. 641; IV, p. 145.

tical needs created by the increase in numbers and the death of the apostles. And here we notice that the Pauline epistles show how a considerable amount of social factors were taken over. These general "human" and social situations were adopted as quite natural and obvious, and then "baptized" by the instruction to do all things "in the Lord"—that is, they were simply put in the perspective of Christ and his Church. Nevertheless, the community had both the right and the duty to eliminate evil-doers from its midst and to smooth out internal conflicts (1 Cor. 5—6). Those who devoted themselves to such work in the community had to be presented "in the Lord" and become a source of respect through exemplary conduct (1 Thess. 5, 12). The community had to test all things, hold on to what was good and avoid every form of evil (1 Thess. 5, 21-22). Its members were required to seek "what is noble in the eyes of all men" and thus, by their conduct, "heap coals" on the head of the enemy (Rom. 12, 17-21). Thus natural social principles were integrated in the life of the community as ways of "good conduct". On the other hand, the members were instructed to "keep away from any of the brothers who refuse to work or to live according to the tradition" passed on to them (2 Thess. 3, 6-12). Those who were receiving instruction were always to "contribute something to the support of the man who was instructing them" (Gal. 6, 6). One should assess in the same way what 1 Timothy 2, 9-15 says about the attitudes, position and function of women. These words simply reflect the general outlook of Hellenistic culture as well as that of Judaism (with reference to Genesis 3, 13). These indications cannot be taken as specifically Christian. They rather reflect the general ideas of social behavior prevailing at that time. There is hardly a virtue or vice which the Christians did not take over in their morality.[10]

The scope of this article does not leave room to show how the question of divorce and the prohibition for a divorcee to remarry (Mt. 5, 32; 19, 3-9; Mk. 10, 4-12; Lk. 16, 8; 1 Cor. 7, 10-11)

[10] Cf. C. Schneider, *Geistesgeschichte des antiken Christentums* I (Stuttgart, 1954), pp. 492f.

must also be seen against the background of the contemporary social situation.[11] But here, too, theology and Canon Law cannot escape the fact that the indications given in Scripture must be seen in their social context and must therefore now be interpreted in the changed situation of the present age.[12]

From these particular instructions, taken over from the social environment, it was but a small step to the legal sanctioning of a given situation as fitting for Christians. Add to this a juridical definition of those "who devote themselves among you to service, preside over you in the Lord and maintain order among you" and we have a formula for the organization of the community. It is therefore only too easy to understand that the "presidents" or "overseers" (*episkopoi*) and helpers (*diakonoi*), addressed for the first time as such in Philippians 1, 1, are more clearly described in the (later) pastoral epistles. But here again it has to be stated that the word *episkopos* was commonly used in public law, common law and the law for associations. In dependent cities this referred to the officials sent to supervise them by the central authority; in independent cities the members of the college of magistrates were called by this name, as were important officeholders in an association.[13]

There is no doubt that when particular circumstances of a domestic or external nature threatened the existence and the meaning of the tradition that had been handed down, the Christian communities were led to adopt also those social and legal regulations and institutions which surrounded them and which seemed appropriate for the preservation of both their nature and their message. Only afterward did these principles become juridical norms and the authority of the leader of the community

---

[11] Cf. J. Dupont, *Mariage et divorce dans l'Evangile* (Bruges, 1959).

[12] For instances of this, see J. Neumann, "Erwägungen zur Revision des kirchlichen Gesetzbuches," in *Theol. Quartalschr.* 146 (1966), p. 217; P. Huizing, "The Indissolubility of Marriage and Church Order," in *Concilium* 38 (1968), pp. 45-57; V. Steininger, *Auflösbarkeit unauflöslicher Ehen* (Graz, 1968); J. Ratzinger, "Zur Theologie der Ehe," in *Theol. Quartalschr.* 149 (1969), pp. 71-73.

[13] Instead of a whole list of references, see *Der Kleine Pauly* II (Stuttgart, 1967), p. 323.

become an office in the juridical sense. Understood in this light, the juridical structures of the early communities grew on the one hand out of the contemporary social and juridical situations of their environment, while, on the other, they showed the practice of the community's faith in the concrete circumstances of life.[14]

There is no room here to show how this process developed by detailed references to the apostolic Fathers [15] and the various Church orders (the *Didache,* the *Didaskalia,* and Hippolytus' *Apostolic Tradition*). In studying these one can see how different social factors and ideas of organization led in the different regions of Syria, Asia Minor and Rome to equally different patterns of Church order. Moreover, often some very concrete cause imposed a particular line and became decisive for the further development of the Church's life. By way of illustration, it is impossible to imagine how the Western Church would have developed if the North African communities, led by Carthage which was very conscious of its importance as an episcopal see, had not perished toward the end of the 7th century. On the other hand, the Church, greatly influenced by the Roman lawyer Tertullian, who came from this same Carthage, took over not only the concepts of Roman law on essential points but even its terminology. The Western theology of the sacraments is still stamped with the fact that Tertullian translated *mysterion,* a Greek word familiar in religious circles, by *sacramentum,* which was an accepted term in Roman law.[16] While the first letter of Clement explained things with juridical concepts, the struggle with the anarchy of gnosticism was waged mainly with juridical weapons. Irenaeus particularly, at the end of the 2nd century, tried to provide the Church with a juridical and legal founda-

[14] Cf. H. W. Bartsch, *Die Anfänge urchristlicher Rechtsbildungen* (Hamburg/Bergstedt, 1965), p. 23 and *passim.*

[15] Cf. J. Neumann, "Der theologische Grund für das kirchliche Vorsteheramt nach dem Zeugnis der Apostolischen Väter," in *Münchener Theol. Zeitschr.* 14 (1963), pp. 253-65, esp. p. 254.

[16] Cf. H. Dombois, *Das Recht der Gnade* (Witten, 1961), pp. 132-39; S. Otto, *"Natura" und "Dispositio". Untersuchung zum Naturbegriff und zur Denkform Tertullians* (Munich, 1960); A. Beck, *Römisches Recht bei Tertullian und Cyprian* (Aalen, 1967).

tion. His teaching of tradition clearly shows that it originated in the tradition of Roman administrative law. The idea of a primacy with a supra-episcopal jurisdiction, like that of the bishop of Rome, could only grow out of this kind of teaching.[17]

No less important for the organization of Church discipline is the fact that early Christianity took root mainly in the Roman empire—that is, in a world molded by Roman law. And it is equally important that Christianity became politically and socially significant only after Diocletian had cast off the last shackles of imperial government and replaced it systematically by an absolute monarchy. He did this because new cultural, political, economic and social forces had emerged and had changed the spiritual and material living conditions of the population of the empire.[18] And when, with Constantine, the bishops not only enjoyed great moral prestige but were also called upon to exercise wide powers of arbitration (*episcopalis audientia*) in civil matters, it became both obvious and inevitable that the Church's organization was decisively influenced by the law of the State.[19] When the Roman empire declined in the West, the Church was the only organization which could take an independent stand against the institutions in the absolute State while at the same time supplementing the State's activities. When under the pressure of the mass migrations the Western sector of the Roman empire finally collapsed, the Church not only could offer the strength of faith and the personal integrity of her leaders, but also could strengthen the heritage of Roman law in order to overcome the prevailing chaos. Church order as well as the formulation of theological cases is therefore unintelligible, even today, without this basic influence of Roman law. Key concepts

[17] Cf. J. Lawson, *The Biblical Theology of St. Irenaeus* (London, 1948).

[18] Cf. M. Kaser, *Römische Rechtsgeschichte* (Göttingen, ²1967), pp. 199 and 217.

[19] This is clear from the fact that the Church's organizational distribution was adjusted to that of the empire (especially in the East) and its terms adopted (diocese, eparchy, *parochia*, etc.). Cf. W. M. Plöchl, *Geschichte des Kirchenrechts* I (Vienna, ²1960), p. 154; *Der Kleine Pauly* II, p. 50.

of Canon Law, such as *forum*,[20] *jurisdictio* and *ordo*, are concepts of Roman law. The *centralized supreme* character of the administration of justice, as implied in the Roman notion of *jurisdictio*,[21] has without any doubt molded the institutions of Church government and their functions, particularly in the Latin Church.

For the hierarchical classification and the separate status of the clergy, the Roman legal concept of *ordo* was probably decisive. *Ordo* meant a closed corporation with very definite rights and duties and a special place in society.[22] The highest *ordo* comprised the members of the Roman Senate. When Canon Law today not only embodies a graded *ordo* among the clergy, but even divides the college of cardinals, the "senate of the Roman pontiff" (c. 230), into three *ordines* (c. 231), we have there a continuation of the Roman juridical *ordo*. This way of thinking in terms of Roman law was curiously linked with Eastern ideas. The work which has had the most enduring influence on the shaping of the ecclesiastical organization in practice, is *About the Church's Hierarchy* by Denys the Areopagite.[23] Here a Christian Orthodox clerical spirituality, based on a faith seen through the filter of a revelation polarized by rational philosophy, is presented in a comprehensive and brilliant way. Against the background of the latent conflict between clergy and monks (particularly in the East)—that is, between "officials" and

[20] Cf. B. Fries, *Forum in der Rechtssprache* (Munich, 1963).

[21] Cf. A. Steinwenter, "Iurisdictio," in *Paulys Realencyclopädie d. class. Altertumswiss.* XIX (Stuttgart, 1894), pp. 1155f.; M. van de Kerkhove, "De notione Jurisdictionis in Jure Romano," in *Ius Pontif.* 16 (1936), pp. 49-65; A. Dumas, "Juridiction ecclésiastique," in *Dict. Droit Can.* VI (Paris, 1957), pp. 236-83, esp. pp. 238-44.

[22] Cf. B. Kübler, "Ordo," in *Paulys Realencyclopädie* XXXV, pp. 930-4; Sachers, "Ordo," in *op. cit.*, Suppl. VII, pp. 792-97; Schnorr von Carolsfeld, *Geschichte der juristischen Person* I (Munich, 1933), pp. 213 and 362.

[23] Up until 1895 the *Peri tes ekklesiastikes hierarchias* was taken as an authentic work of Denys the Areopagite of Athens. It is now certain that it cannot have been written before 482: see W. Fritsch, in H. Ball, *Die Hierarchien der Angel und der Kirche* (Munich/Planegg, 1955), p. 7; B. Altaner, *Patrologie* (Freiburg, ⁶1960), pp. 466-70.

"charismatics" (with a gnosticizing tendency), Denys extols the priestly ideal to the utmost. The priestly functions are hierarchically ordered. The hierarch is divine and moved by God; like the apostles and the prophets he proclaims the divine judgment and announces divine visions; he shares in the service of the angels. The monks move at a wholly different level; they are still struggling with the profanities of the world, are still living in alien parts, and are still caught up in the dualism of good and evil. Only angels and priests proclaim the revealed Word, not the monks. The "hierarchy is a God-founded science", "a position inspired by the exemplar of God himself". It is "the system which embraces all available factors of salvation, according to our venerable tradition". "Among the ranks of those who see God", the hierarch occupies the highest and most divine rank. He is filled with "the power of perfection".[24] However much this outlook of Denys may differ from the Roman one, this apotheosis of the priesthood as the rank and status of a God-founded knowledge easily fits in with the juridical quality of the *ordo,* and it is only one step from the mystical "power of perfection" of the hierarch to the *plena potestas* (full power) and *jurisdictio* of Roman law.

It is therefore easy to pass from Denys to Gregory VII and Boniface VIII, not to mention other names. As history shows, however, there is no straight line from the one to the other. The development took place in a roundabout way. The prevailing situation at that time had to meet the Germanic invasion with new morals and new ideas about law, and this new force had enormous consequences.[25]

A series of legal institutions, totally alien to ecclesiastical administration and theology, found their way into ecclesiastical

[24] Migne, *PG* III, cc. 370-570, esp. 505a-d: *"Estin oun hierarchike taxis he tes teleiotikes dunameos anapeplesmene. . . ."* (505c).
[25] We have left out the additional and confusing problem of Celtic and Scottish Christianity. It must be remembered that this means that a further essential factor has not been brought in to make room for important social and juridical factors which needed more space.

practice. To refer only to the two perhaps most important ones, I mention here the *Eigenkirche* (privately owned church) and the system of *benefices*. The idea that a church building could belong to an owner other than the Church—e.g., a bishop or a monastery—was uncommon for a long time. But that services taking place in such a building could be financially "exploited" was unthinkable.

The system of *Eigenkirchen,* which made the landowners the proprietors of the church on their soil and which developed in the 6th and 7th centuries, led to that medieval feudalism which was decisive for the structures of both Church and State. The ecclesiastical function itself, closely linked with its appropriate revenue, the "benefice", became the object of bargaining.[26] Only a fierce and protracted struggle saved the Church from being overrun by an un-spiritual system. Even so, the Church was not always victorious. It is also due to this feudal system that one had to belong to a certain class—freemen, or high aristocracy —to be able to assume ecclesiastical office, or even to enter a monastery.[27]

Even ecclesiastical justice in the end adjusted itself to the class system: "Land ownership, with its concomitant features of immunity and official responsibilities, dominated the ecclesiastical institutions, not only with regard to property but also constitutionally and in class law." [28] With the remains of the old Roman law the Cluniac reformers tried to bring about a renewal in

[26] Cf. U. Stuz, *Geschichte des kirchlichen Benefizialwesens von seinen Anfängen bis auf die Zeit Alexander III* (Aalen, [2]1961), esp. pp. 95f.; H. E. Feine, *Kirchliche Rechtsgeschichte* (Cologne/Graz, [4]1964), pp. 147-50; W. M. Plöchl, *Geschichte des Kirchenrechts* I (Vienna/Munich, [2]1960), pp. 426f. For the Church under Roman law, see G. Krüger, *Die Rechtsstellung der vorkonstantinischen Kirchen* (Amsterdam, 1961), esp. pp. 146f.; R. Freudensberger, *Das Verhalten der römischen Behörden gegen die Christen im 2. Jahrhundert* (Munich, 1967); for useful material, see R. Hernegger, *Macht ohne Auftrag* (Freiburg, 1963).
[27] Cf. K. Voigt, *Die karolingische Klosterpolitik und der Niedergang des westfränkischen Königtums. Laienäbte und Klosterinhaber* (Amsterdam, 1965); A. Schulte, *Der Adel und die deutsche Kirche im Mittelalter* (Amsterdam, 1966).
[28] H. E. Feine, *op. cit.,* p. 149.

the spirit of the older law, but they did not succeed in eliminating all the effects of Germanic legal concepts. This struggle continues to this very day.

Why this long—and yet too short—historical introduction? Certainly it is not to show that everything went wrong in the past. Only those without a sense of history set themselves up as judges of their ancestors. But we ought to learn two lessons from this history.

1. The juridical order of the Church "grew" out of various social presuppositions. It therefore contains historically conditioned norms which, in another historical situation, may not only have become antiquated, but even detrimental. Every disciplinary measure must therefore be understood in the light of its origin. We then have to ask whether the original purpose of the measure can still be attained today by the same means, and whether such a measure is still legitimate today, given the Church's mandate. Much has been allowed, naturally and discreetly, to fall into desuetude, such as the foundations of the high aristocracy and the original principles of the system of benefices. Other things, however, have been retained, although no less conditioned by the social concepts of their historical origin, such as various forms of organization like the territorial parish and, connected with this, the detailed rules about parochial baptism and burial.

2. The second point might well be that the understanding of the limited and time-conditioned character of many norms ought to make us beware of overrating the importance and permanence of our own views and the laws we lay down accordingly. It should make us beware particularly of overlooking some basic principles of justice and equity. Pastoral utility should never lead to a neglect of these basic principles of justice and fairness. That this is still the case in the Code of Canon Law of 1918 to the detriment of the reputation of Canon Law and the ecclesiastical authority behind it is not difficult to prove.

While it is true that the Church is by no means merely a social body and can therefore not be treated solely as a sociological object, history also shows that the Church cannot ignore the social situation of the world in which she operates. Today this means that the Church must mold her order in such a way that her saving service remains possible and is not hampered in a world that has undergone basic social changes. The organization or order of the Church must therefore concentrate on those principles that man has become only recently aware of as basic values and that are most endangered in a technological consumer and group society—namely, the dignity and freedom of every human person as the image of God. If the Church were today again, as at the collapse of the Roman empire, to become the bulwark of the defense of man, taking into account the varying situations in the various parts of the world, she would certainly not be untrue to the legacy with which she has been entrusted. She would, however, be untrue to her mission if, in this changed world with its incredible needs and risks and its never before imagined opportunities for building as for destruction, she would refuse to reexamine her whole disciplinary order. Two examples may clarify this.

1. Since very early times it was common practice to baptize infants on the basis of their parents' faith and consent. Sacramental baptism makes a person subject to all the rights and duties of a Christian. When it was natural for a person to grow up in the ecclesiastical community, this practice may well have been justified as a regulation of Canon Law. But today this can no longer be taken for granted by any means. If we wish to maintain this infant baptism—and there are theological arguments for doing so—then the acceptance of the rights and duties implied in baptism must be juridically deferred to a fixed age and made dependent on a free decision of the will of the person who has been baptized, particularly since grave consequences are involved in law. As in every other field, Church order must accept the fact that society and social assumptions have undergone a basic change.

2. Just as in early times the Church and the respective local

churches were "governed" according to the notion of sovereign *jurisdictio,* and in the Middle Ages "ruled" according to feudal principles, so today, in the age of *participation,* a genuine collegial-fraternal management is required. Here the Church order must be concerned with her aptitude for such guidance of the community and do all she can to equip the person for collaboration. Finally, she must take account of the theological and social changes that have affected the image of the priest and adapt it to the specific living conditions of man in an industrial age. Parochial coercion, as it existed up till now, and the old territorial organization of the parish have become impossible.

Only when Canon Law faces up to the social and factual changes that have brought about a spiritual revolution in mankind—a revolution from which the Church is not exempt—can the Church achieve her purpose as described by Pius XII: "The Church should always and everywhere form man, individually and collectively, according to the law of Christ by constant adaptation to the actual conditions of time and place, for it is in this way that she penetrates into the moral foundations of the living community. The aim of the Church is man, who is good by nature and who, filled with Christ's truth and grace, is ennobled and strengthened thereby." [29] Canon Law should always remember that the order and development of the community must always take its cue from the good of the person, for the order of things must serve the order of persons and not vice versa. This statement of Vatican Council II [30] also applies to the Church. Just as the social order constantly develops, so the Church's order must be rooted in truth, built up in justice and animated by love, and so constantly try to find an increasingly humane balance in freedom.[31] "An improvement in attitudes and widespread changes in society will have to take place if these

[29] Address given to the 10th International Congress of Historians on Sept. 7, 1955 (quoted from *Herder-Korrespondenz* 10, p. 75).

[30] *Constitution on the Church in the Modern World,* n. 26.

[31] John XXIII, *Pacem in Terris,* in *AAS* 55 (1963), p. 266, quoted in the *Constitution on the Church in the Modern World,* n. 26.

objectives are to be gained." [32] And this, without any doubt, holds equally true for the "society" of the Church, for where else would the apostle's words find their application: "Where the Spirit of the Lord governs, there is freedom" (2 Cor. 3, 17)?

[32] *Constitution on the Church in the Modern World*, n. 26.

Wilhelm Steinmüller/*Regensburg, West Germany*

Divine Law and Its Dynamism in Protestant Theology of Law

T he pervasive dynamization of every area of life is the hallmark of the present day. Never before in history has it gripped society to this degree. This process began in the Renaissance, picked up steam in the heyday of classical capitalism, and is now evident to everyone. It will keep on accelerating in the future, unless we manage to institutionalize forces that will harness and control it.

I

THE CHALLENGE CONFRONTING CHURCH LAW

This current dynamization involves several phenomena. First of all, it involves the *acceleration* of many social processes and, perhaps, the end of a static world view. Along with this acceleration goes the continuing transformation of society's constituent structures, including its regulatory systems (ethics, morals, law,[1] institutions). It becomes more and more impossible to handle this situation with static approaches.[2]

[1] R. F. Behrendt's remarks on the sociological changes in the notion of virtue also hold true for the notion of law. See R. F. Behrendt, "Tugenden von gestern und für morgen," in *Futurum* 1 (1968), pp. 23-49.

[2] For example, by stressing authority or such secondary virtues as calmness, security and order; or by fearfully enacting hidebound laws that try to eliminate the element of uncertainty in any given area.

25

Since this process moves forward at varying degrees of speed and breaks off in different directions, it produces an intensified degree of *pluralism* within and between various social groups. Protecting and guaranteeing the freedom of minorities, once a peripheral problem, now becomes a central issue.

Our present dynamized society is the takeoff point for this article, for such a society needs a legal system that is flexible enough to embrace this acceleration and pluralism in an *elastic framework of freedom*.[3] Since the Church cannot stand aloof from human society, she too must face the problem. She needs a *dynamic Church law* that is capable of merging respect for the past with the requirements of the future; only then can she prevent a radical break with tradition.

Can such dynamism be regulated? Whatever we may answer, it is obvious that law must remain law. It cannot disintegrate into actualistic, existentialistic or personalistic whim. Most importantly, it cannot be based on uncritical adoption of worldly structures. Its dynamism must be grounded in the true nature of the Church, and it must be limited and legitimized by divine law.[4] This means that we must draw a clearer distinction between *ius divinum* and *ius humanum,* penetrating more deeply into the exact nature of each. Thus contemporary Catholic Church law faces two urgent tasks: it must gain a deeper knowledge of the *nature* and *dynamism* of divine and human Church law.

II

PROTESTANT THEOLOGY OF LAW: THREE PRESENTATIONS

In this connection we shall examine a new discipline that arose out of the confrontation between German Christians and the rulers of the Third Reich. Originated by Protestants, it is called

---

[3] Freedom, in this sense, would make dialogue possible within the Church and a pluralistic society. See K. Rahner, *Schriften zur Theologie* VI (Einsiedeln-Zurich-Cologne, 1965), pp. 34ff. and 46ff.

[4] "Divine law" and *ius divinum* are used synonymously in this article.

theology of law.[5] It has no ready-made answers to offer us, of course, since it has been primarily concerned with other issues up to now. But in the three major theories to be presented here we shall find noteworthy viewpoints [6] that lead to closely related conclusions despite their different terminology and starting points.[7]

Johannes Heckel

The law theory of Johannes Heckel grew out of his exploration into Luther's views on law [8]—the latter growing out of

[5] Theology of law (*Rechtstheologie*) has already become the *terminus technicus* for that discipline which deals with the theological foundations of law. For its precise differentiation from Church law, see W. Steinmüller, "Rechtstheologie und Kirchenrecht als theologische Disziplinen mit juristischer Methode," in *Ius Sacrum* (Paderborn, 1969), pp. 846-60. For older Protestant theology of law, see K. L. Schlaich, *Kollegialismus: Die Kirche und ihr Recht in der Zeit der Aufklärung* (Tübingen); H. Fagerberg, *Bekenntnis, Kirche und Amt in der deutschen konfessionellen Theologie des 19. Jahrhunderts* (Uppsala, 1952); C. Link, *Die Grundlagen der Kirchenverfassung im lutherischen Konfessionalismus des 19. Jahrhunderts* (Munich, 1966). On Catholic theology of law, especially the Spanish version, see the bibliographical references in the following articles: L. De Echeverría, "The Theology of Canon Law," in *Concilium* 28 (1967), pp. 7-15; Teodoro Jiménez-Urresti, "Canon Law And Theology: Two Different Sciences," in *Concilium* 28 (1967), pp. 17-26. For German viewpoints, see the bibliography in the work of Steinmüller cited in footnote 6. On the complicated problem confronting German Christians, see E. Klügel, "Deutsche Christen," and H. Brunotte, "Kirchenkampf," in *Evangelisches Kirchenlexicon* I ([2]1962), pp. 868-71; II ([2]1962), pp. 737-49.

[6] The theories briefly sketched in this article and the reasons why they were selected may be found in the work of this author that is cited in the previous footnote (see pp. 849ff.). For an even fuller presentation with bibliography, see W. Steinmüller, *Evangelische Rechtstheologie*, 2 vols. (Cologne-Graz, 1968).

[7] Quite obviously, one must take great care in trying to transfer Protestant ideas and conclusions over into Catholic questions and problems. One must allow for reservations, since all the terms used (Church, grace, Spirit, law, existence, etc.) are empty formulas, to which each author gives a different content. For the methodology used in transferring between these different systems, see *ibid.*, I, pp. 9ff. and II, pp. 791ff. I have tried to hint at the linguistic style of each author in my presentation within this paper.

[8] Heckel's treatment of Luther is interesting in two respects. It is undeniably a major contribution to historical research on Luther by the man who knew his juridical thought better than anyone else. Heckel died in

Luther's disagreement with Canon Law. The notion of a "non-juridical Luther" (H. Liermann) must be rejected as a fairy tale: "Luther's doctrine of law is a component part of his theology; it is a theological doctrine of law."

The center of Luther's law doctrine is the doctrine of the two kingdoms, which is the working out of God's plan of justification for mankind. The "labyrinthine doctrine of the two kingdoms" holds the key to Luther's doctrine of law, Church and State. According to Heckel, it contains two basic elements: the doctrine of the two kingdoms and the doctrine of the two "regiments" (i.e., systems of government).[9]

The *two kingdoms* are a necessary consequence of God's summons to mankind. The person who believes belongs to Christ's kingdom; the person who remains fast in unbelief belongs to the kingdom of the world. The kingdom of Christ is subject to Christ's kingly rule, and everything in it is tightly and "personally" tied to him. The kingdom of the world, under the lordship of Satan, represents the complete shadow side and caricature of Christ's kingdom.

These two kingdoms are locked in bitter conflict until the end of the world. This would cause the ruination of creation, except for the fact that God's two governments (i.e., his lordship over both kingdoms) prevent this catastrophe. The "spiritual government" (regiment) directs the kingdom of Christ, while the "worldly government" guides the kingdom of the world. The former operates through Christ's Gospel, using the ministry of

---

1963. It is also a very updated exercise in contemporary theology of law and Church law study; it is of first-rate ecumenical importance, as his pupil, S. Grundmann (d. 1966), has shown. It is the latter aspect that interests us here.

[9] This topic has already been given an excellent treatment in *Concilium*. See J. van Laarhoven, "The Origin of Luther's Doctrine of the Two Kingdoms," *Concilium* 17 (1966), pp. 50-62. For another view, see H. H. Schrey, "Beyond Natural Law and Positivism," in *Concilium* 25 (1967), pp. 59-73 (Heckel is treated on pp. 70-71). By contrast, the traditional Lutheran doctrine of the two kingdoms equates the "kingdom" with departmentalized "regiments", so that the Christian (contra Heckel) is subject to both regiments; this leads to the well-known Lutheran position on subordination to the State.

Word and sacrament; the latter operates through God's "law" and compulsion, using the office of authority. In this way God makes even the worldly kingdom serve his divine plan, and he preserves Christ's kingdom from certain ruination.

Thus the dualism of the two kingdoms and the two governments is not absolute and complete. The unifying point is God's one and only plan of law and love for all mankind. Blame for the split rests squarely on man's shoulders.

The doctrine of the two kingdoms is clarified and exemplified by the theological doctrine of law. The two doctrines form a unity. The latter is only one component part of the former, and both together represent a theological anthropology in medieval dress.

The starting point is God's one plan of law, which is identical with his plan of love. It finds expression in two types of law: God's natural law and the founding of two proto-institutions. In the beginning God's natural law was spoken to the hearts of all men. After it had been obscured by sin, it was again interpreted authentically by Christ (as *lex Christi*) and restored to its pristine sense as the *lex caritatis spiritualis*. If a person accepts God's natural law by faith and recognizes its binding force, he belongs to the kingdom of Christ. God's natural law, the *lex Christi,* is identical with the legal order embodied in Christ's kingdom. God's plan of law also finds expression in the creation of two proto-institutions, the Church and marriage, which provide relationship to God and to the opposite sex.

The worldly kingdom and its citizens reject God's natural law internally, and they misread it "externally" as "worldly natural law". Worldly natural law is therefore identical with the false interpretation of God's natural law by fallen man in the kingdom of the world.[10] A similar perversion affects the two proto-institutions.[11]

The result is a paradoxical state of affairs. Because of man's

[10] Contrary to popular belief, we must point out that Luther sees law as ontologically possible even for fallen man. "Naturalia sunt integra, concedo," he notes, in his 1531 commentary on the Epistle to the Galatians (Weimar edition, XL 1, 293, 7). Only man's ties with God are

acceptance or rejection of faith, God's one plan of law and love gives rise to the "eschatological antithesis" (Ernst Wolf) of kingdom and law. And from this moderately dualistic doctrine of the two kingdoms there derives a moderately dualistic doctrine of natural law.

Other basic notions in Heckel's theory of law can be outlined quickly. His *doctrine of Church and State* is again a component part of the doctrine of the two kingdoms. The kingdom of Christ is identical with the "spiritual Church". It lives in the world as a universal "physical" or "earthly" Church, organized as member churches. In God's sight, the spiritual Church and the physical Church are personally identical; in man's incomplete and short-sighted view, a chasm separates the two.[12] The State, on the other hand, is personally identical with the kingdom of the world, though it is organized under God's worldly government.[13]

Accordingly, Church law and worldly law are merely incomplete and dependent constituents of the legal order of both kingdoms. Since Christ's kingdom is one with the spiritual Church, the latter can have only one Church law: the *ius divinum* of Christ's kingdom. It is composed of two parts: the *ius divinum positivum* of the Church that was created anew by Christ, and

---

"totally corrupted", with consequent effects upon man's relations with his neighbor.

[11] The primitive Church was perverted into a government-type Church right up to the present day. Marriage was converted into an "external, physcial thing". The home rule of the father has degenerated into a coercive authoritarian force, which God utilizes in the worldly regime. Thus marriage, tainted by original sin, becomes the nucleus of the State.

[12] The unbelieving baptized are only seeming members of the earthly Church (note Heckel's use of the Augustinian formula: they are *in ecclesia, non de ecclesia; numero, non merito; specie, non re vera*) and belong therefore to the kingdom of the world. Contrary to Augustine, then, the Church is not a *civitas permixta* of believers and unbelievers. To be sure, because of the spiritual character of baptism and our lack of full knowledge, Church membership must be attributed to the unbelieving baptized so long as the contrary is not made evident by clear-cut serious sins.

[13] For Lutheranism, this is the "revolutionary" (S. Grundmann) Janus aspect of the State "between Romans 13 and Apocalypse 13" (*idem*).

the *ius divinum naturale* of spiritual brotherly love. The spiritual Church, then, lives exclusively according to divine law.

The universal Church (through her member churches), on the other hand, carries out this twofold divine law through a two-fold human Church law. Thus she lives exclusively according to basic human law—although on the foundation of divine law. Similarly, positive State law is based on the perverted version of divine law in the kingdom of the world—i.e., on worldly natural law.

Erik Wolf

At first glance the inner framework of Erik Wolf's theology of law would seem to be wholly different from that of Heckel. It is a multi-layered theology, combining neo-Kantian ideas with elements of existential philosophy (E. Grisebach, M. Heidegger and S. Kierkegaard), the experiences of the confessing Church, and insights of Karl Barth. The result is an original "dialectical" theology of law that avoids extremes and concentrates on the Bible's guiding message. It proclaims "Christocracy" and "brotherhood".

Christ the Lord, in whom all things have been created, is the ruler of the whole world, and in faith we can experience this Christocracy. Christ is also true man, who makes authentic (i.e., Christian) brotherhood possible. Because Christ's lordship is really service to one's brother, as we learn from the cross, it is a "brotherly Christocracy". And because authentic human brotherhood is made existentially possible through Christ's lordship, it is "Christocratic brotherhood".

Man learns about Christocracy and brotherhood through the Word of God, the Bible's guiding message. It is God's plan of law revealed in Christ. Because of its origin, it is absolutely binding; it is (non-normative) "law" of a particular sort, an evangelical *ius divinum*.

This twofold basic structure of "vertical" Christocracy and

"horizontal" brotherhood is also the primary characteristic of "Christian existence"—a central concept in Wolf's theological-juridical anthropology. The second hallmark of Christian existence is the "acute paradox" of man—existentially still a sinner, yet truly redeemed in Christ. The third characteristic of Christian existence is its unrelinquishably communitarian nature, which involves a fundamental dialectic between "happening" (the gathering together that takes place continually) and "institution" (that which is already given from the start since Christ). Christian existence is ecclesial existence.[14]

Once we have these three elements of Christian existence, we have the Church. Paradoxical Christian existence is ecclesial existence. The basic structure of the Church is composed of the three elements of Christian existence that we have already mentioned; hence it is a by-product of divine law (in Wolf's sense). The Church is constituted formally through the Word of God —i.e., the Bible's guiding message. Her makeup is circumscribed materially through the vertical reality of brotherly Christocracy and the horizontal reality of Christocentric brotherhood. Christocracy and brotherhood are realized primarily in the dialectic between fixed "knowledge" of the faith and existential "profession" of the faith by the community of God's people—a community that exists in dialectical tension "between" sin and redemption.

The Church's ius humanum rests upon the same threefold basic structure. Thus human Church law is established and limited formally by the ius divinum of the Bible's guiding message, and materially by Christocracy and brotherhood. The Christocracy is proclaimed by preaching, baptism and the eucharist—i.e., by worship of God. Church law, then, is first and foremost an "order devoted to divine worship". It is equally an "order of service", for Christocracy becomes an interpersonal reality in brotherhood. Finally, it is also a "paradoxical order" governing a Church that is simultaneously sin-ridden and redeemed. In the face of the world, however, Church law is a "professing" and

[14] This leads Wolf to reject actualistic existentialism.

"example-giving" law (containing the dialectic of happening and institution) in dialectical opposition to the civil order of law.

Hans Dombois

We enter another world when we approach the theory of Hans Dombois and his "law of grace". In his theology of law, worship of God again occupies the central place. In a never-ending dialogue and debate with that great master and opponent of Church law, Rudolph Sohm, Dombois works up an original theory of law and institutions [15] that is ingenious in many respects and that also borrows elements from the law theory of the Eastern Churches.

Dombois' juridical anthropology is built upon two bases: (1) a doctrine of the Trinity that is influenced by Karl Barth and that views Christ wholly in terms of the Council of Chalcedon; (2) a "trinitarian" theological anthropology which contains much more eschatology than one would expect from a jurist. He explains human life as an "existence" with a typical "structure" that operates in "historical" and "personal" "relations".

With the help of these basic concepts, Dombois sets forth his theory of institutions. Of the many possible relations, there are four "basic relations" that are the most comprehensive: man's relation to God, to the opposite sex, to his fellow man, and to the objective world. By virtue of the perduring "structure" of "existential" activity, the actual implementation of each basic relationship leads necessarily to an institution. Dombois follows each basic relationship through to its corresponding institution, presenting us with the four basic institutions of a "personal" nature: the Church, marriage, the State and property. All these basic institutions have a typical bi-partite structure: they are the dynamic "historical" process of entering a particular "status".

[15] We cannot treat all the contributing influences here. Let us just mention a few of them: epistemological reflections; the phenomenology of G. van der Leeuw; the anthropological and sociological theory of institutions proposed by A. Gehlen and H. Schelsky; the integration theory of R. Smend; the concrete law theory of C. Schmitt. Dombois also develops a special "complementary" line of thought that works with "implied definitions" (taken over from modern logic).

From there Dombois goes on to develop his "institutional" doctrine of *law*. Viewed philosophically, law is simply the typical structure of man's personal, institutionalizing activity in various relationships; in other words, it is to be identified with the structure of the institutionalizing process. This leads to the wondrous discovery of grace as a law process. Law and legal structures, analogous to those found in the four basic institutions, are to be found in the theological process of justification (i.e., redemption) as well as in the juridical process of pardon. Grace (in both the theological and juridical sense) is not an irregular breach of law; rather, it is an institutionalizing law process that can be spelled out in precise juridical terms.

Our customary *normative law,* on the other hand, emerges as a secondary and complementary area of law. It, too, must be viewed as an historical, interrelational happening between persons—specifically, as a process of recognizing claims upon us.

Dombois' theory of Church and Church law proceeds from his theory of law and institution. The Church is simply a particular instance of institution. She is the institution *par excellence,* the institutional form of man's relationship to God. She too arises from (divine and) human activity. She is the natural, historical continuation of Christ's institutionalizing activity, in which he places man before God in a new status—i.e., as redeemed. The process is continued in man's worship of God. Through Word and sacrament, the spiritual *institutio* of man becomes a reality. In worship of God, the Church becomes a reality.

Church law, too, comes into existence through divine worship. As the law of justifying grace, it is a particular instance of institutional law; indeed, it is the institutional law *par excellence.* It is formally identical with the legal structure of Christ's institutional activity; it is materially identical with the legal structure of divine worship, which receives and hands on Christ's activity in history. Thus the law of professing the Word is identical with the legal structure of the proclamation process in its various forms (preaching, teaching, dogma formation, etc.), and liturgical or sacramental law is identical with the legal structure of sacramental administration (baptism, the eucharist, and the *sacramentum spiritus sancti* as the sum of the other sacraments).

III
ESSENTIAL POINTS OF SIMILARITY

Despite the unfamiliar concepts and lines of thought, the three theories sketched above show surprising agreement on themes related to our present topic. We shall examine two basic themes here.

Divine and Human Church Law

Let us first consider the difference between divine and human Church law. In Heckel's theory, divine law is identical with the government of Christ the head over the members of his kingdom. As the proto-law, it embraces "nature" and "grace" and it effects the justification (redemption) of sinners. As *ius divinum* it establishes and maintains the spiritual Church, and thus becomes the legal foundation for the *ius humanum* of the earthly Church.

Human Church law, on the other hand, is merely the earthly side of divine Church law in the earthly Church. It can be the declaratory exposition of the founder's will in Word, sacrament and the power of the keys ("heteronomous" Church law), or the Church order established by men in other respects for the sake of brotherly love ("autonomous" Church law). On the one hand, therefore, human Church law is the concrete earthly form of existence taken by eschatological divine law; it is *Christological law,* because *extra Christum nullum ius* (Heckel). On the other hand, human Church law is "out and out beggary" because it is existentially jeopardized by sin.

Thus divine and human Church law bear the same relationship to each other as does the spiritual Church (i.e., Christ's kingdom) to the fragile earthly Church. They must be sharply distinguished from one another. They are not to be split off from one another, nor are they to be mixed together.

We find similar ideas in the theory of Erik Wolf. Christian (i.e., ecclesial) existence is characterized by the union of God's Word (i.e., the Bible's guiding message) and its divine law with the unerasable sinfulness of the redeemed. Human Church law is the paradoxical ordering of this paradox. Thus between *ius divinum* and *ius humanum* there exists an acute *dialectic*, described by Wolf as "unity in difference".

The element of difference is this: Not only must human Church law take account of the concrete sinfulness of Christian existence, but it itself is set up and carried out by sinful men. The element of unity is grounded on the function of divine law, which is to be the ground, limit and goal of all human legal dispositions.

The issue is more difficult for H. Dombois, since he expressly rejects the Catholic normative understanding of *ius divinum*. At the same time he does espouse an evangelical *ius divinum*, which takes the form of "perduring legal structures" in divine and human activity through history. The process begins with the Old Testament covenant. It reaches its high point in Christ's institutionalizing activity, whereby he installs his disciples in the new status of salvation. Finally, the process is carried forward in history through the worshiping community's activities of proclaiming the Word and celebrating the sacraments. In all these *legal forms of grace*, which are structurally equivalent, the Spirit of God communicates itself to mankind and empowers it to undertake new spiritual activity.

Dombois goes on to spell out the tieup and the distinction between *ius divinum* and *ius humanum*. They are to be found in the fact that (1) divine and human activity evince "similar" legal structures, while (2) human activity is tied up with God's activity, and is only made possible within the grace-filled legal process of divine justification. On the one hand we can say that "God (or Christ) is both the subject and object of Church law"

—i.e., that he is the only object and operator in the process. On the other hand, we can also say what seems to be the exact opposite: that God operates solely through the historical medium of human activity and its legal structure.

The Dynamism of Church Law

The dynamism of Church law is closely tied up with our understanding of *ius divinum*. Dynamic human law is only possible because and insofar as divine law is dynamic—i.e., insofar as it leaves plenty of room for freedom to grow in.

In Heckel's theory, *ius divinum* is endowed with divine dynamism. For it is essentially "nothing but Spirit", the Spirit of Christ, the redeeming *lex Christi*.[16] As such it is the perfect *lex universalis*, which normatively regulates the general and concretely regulates the particular.[17] It is all-embracing and indivisible in the Spirit of love.

Despite the gap which separates the two, human Church law participates in this active impulse. Autonomous Church law is wholly a creation of brotherly love. It is valid as "pedagogical law" only where it is beneficial to the faith of our brothers; in instances where it is injurious to our brothers, it is not to be observed. Thus it is an elastic reality, capable of adapting to changing needs. It is to be gas for the motor, not sand in the carburetor.

At this point we find a further difference between divine Church law and worldly law. Since the divine plan of law calls for acceptance in faith, its legal character comes out only in conjunction with the actual practice of faith—i.e., in *usus spiritualis*

[16] As with Augustine. See Thomas Aquinas, *Summa Theologica*, II/1, q. 106, a. 1c: "Id autem quod est potissimum in lege novi testamenti et in quo tota virtus eius consistit, est gratia Spiritus Sancti"; a. 2c: "Lex nova iustificat; etiam littera Evangelii (= nova lex) occideret, nisi adesset interius gratia fidei sanans." See also G. Söhngen, *Gesetz und Evangelium* (Freiburg-Munich, 1957), pp. 57 and 117; *idem, Grundfragen einer Rechtstheologie* (Munich, 1962), pp. 96ff.

[17] The totalitarian thrust of this overall legalization is toned down by the fact that *ius divinum* in action is identical with the Spirit of Christ, and *ius humanum* does not stand on the same level with it. *Ius humanum* also has the task of preserving the "basic law" of Christian freedom.

iuris. Now this characteristic of divine Church law must be imitated in human law. So human Church law, too, is legally binding only insofar as it is "spiritually" administered in the full clarity of faith. What is more, the three "basic rights" of Christians must be respected: Christian brotherhood, equality in the royal priesthood, and Christian liberty.

Erik Wolf's concept of law, different though it be, also leads to an "open order". For God's transcendent law over mankind, which makes possible all human law, is the Bible's guiding message. It is the "Word (of God) in the words (of Scripture)" (K. Barth). Or, to put it in other words, it is the living legal kerygma of Scripture which brings justification to man and trains him in the proper use of his new freedom.

Human Church law, accordingly, is also a kerygmatic law of freedom. It is both the formulated *norm* of faith-profession and the actual *fulfillment* of this norm in professing our faith before the world (i.e., the example-giving legal action of love). Thus, by adopting the anthropological proto-dialectic of "institution and happening" (J. L. Leuba) in his concept of law, Wolf is able to provide Church law with an openness toward the free decision of faith and the new stimulus of the Spirit.

Dombois presents his institutional law as a covenant law of freedom and grace in history and salvation history. Since God effects his "existence-grounding law of grace" in the history of the Old Testament covenant and the new People of God, divine and human law are indissolubly associated with the dynamism of salvation history. The "perduring legal structure" of grace and its law must be made real anew in every age through an "existential interpretation of Church law" (but not in Rudolf Bultmann's sense). Each age has its own opportunity and its own failings.

For Dombois, moreover, both the law of grace and normative law represent a "process" of institutionalization and law formation. Hence the formation and revision of law are subsumed into his concept of law as dynamic elements of it. The legal rigidity of abstract, exceptionless norms is resolved by anchoring them in the living, existential, and hence flexible institution.[18]

Law, in both forms, contains a dynamic element of freedom. For grace, according to Dombois, always sets one free—on the legal plane also. The person who is pardoned acquires a new status of freedom, as the baptized babe is inserted into the freedom of God's child and heir. To be sure, there is no freedom without limits. From the proffered grace follow (quasi) normative obligations, whose infringement can entail the loss of grace. The Torah, for example, was originally viewed as an obligatory specification of the contents of the covenant.

Even the legal claims of "normative law" (the second sphere of law) acquire universal binding force only where they are accepted in freedom. This would be the case, for example, when we form a judgment on the qualifications of a candidate for some official office, or on the orthodoxy of some Council. As was the case in the early Church, Church law rests upon free "mutual recognition" (E. Schlinck): "Only the Spirit knows and judges the Spirit."

IV
RELEVANT CONCLUSIONS FOR CANONISTS

Current Protestant theology of law affirms the existence of a *ius divinum*. Its understanding of divine law is achieved and deepened by utilizing the data of theology, history, sociology, philosophy and jurisprudence. In this way it resists the temptation to oversecularize Church law, and the contrary temptation to "overtheologize" (H. Liermann).[19]

One of the main reasons for its avoidance of these temptations

[18] For more on the legal structure of the covenant, see the article by H. Dombois in this volume. Also cf. J. Hoffmann, "Grâce et institution selon Han Dombois," in *Rev. Sc. Phil. Théol.* 52 (1968), pp. 645-76.

[19] The theorists discussed in this paper agree that the Church's law of love must be a "juridical law" too, and that it therefore must satisfy the strict methodological requirements of jurisprudence.

is its recognition of the distinctiveness and relatedness of divine and human law. *Ius divinum* and *ius humanum* are "analogous". They are related to each other as the divine and the human side of the Church.[20]

The first thing we must do is to draw a sharp distinction between them. Since *ius divinum* derives from revelation as God's law for men, it is not "law" in the same sense that human Church law is. The latter, as an analogous law, is *not* law more than it is law. This can be seen most clearly in the fact that human Church law, unlike divine law, does not serve to justify sinners; moreover, it is weighted down with man's inescapable sinfulness. If, by the same token, we designate *ius humanum* as real "law", then *ius divinum* is "transcendent law", more, unlike than like human law.

Despite all this they resemble each other in certain respects. *Ius divinum* is *the* original law; compared with it, *ius humanum* is only a shadow image of law. Because divine Church law is a law of the Spirit, a law of grace and love, the ecclesiastical lawgiver has a corresponding legal obligation to mirror this material structure in his human Church law insofar as he can; thus he will provide a model for the world. Its similarity to divine law, then, is an unending duty more than a ready-made fact.

In the last analysis, divine human law cannot be *intermixed* or *separated* any more than can the divine and human side of the Church. Divine law never exists historically in pure, unadulterated form; it only exists in the "corporeality" of human law, which is thereby changed in turn. For this reason all Church law, even human Church law, is essentially different from the worldly law of governments and peoples.

Finally, Protestant theology of law grounds the *dynamism* of the Church on *ius divinum,* thus making it independent of socie-

---

[20] See *Lumen gentium,* nn. 3 and 8 for the relationship of the Spirit of Christ to the "Church in the world—analogous to the hypostatic union. This relationship is to be complemented and completed by the "Church of sinners" (*Lumen gentium*) n. 8; *Gaudium et spes,* n. 43) and the "ecclesia semper reformanda" (*Lumen gentium,* n. 8, and *Unitatis redintegratio,* nn. 3f. and 6).

tal influences. Church law thereby acquires its own *independent* legal foundation for assimilating societal dynamisms.

Even here, to be sure, the Church remains fast in her *eschatological distance* from the world. Divine law reveals the limits to whatever assimilation of worldly law might take place,[21] thus preventing the oversecularization of the Church. This distance from the world shows up in our three authors insofar as they all feel compelled, on *theological* grounds, to move away from a worldly, one-sided notion of law that would be normative and legalistic. By taking this turn they are able to fashion Church law into an open and flexible order of freedom, an order which leaves room for a pluralistic Church and for the dynamism of the Spirit (who blows where he wills).

Hopefully an independent Catholic theology of law, learning well from discussions with its Protestant counterpart and utilizing its twofold theological and juridical methodology, will provide us with new solutions for the central problems facing the Church.

[21] Because of its historical origins (i.e., as an antidote to an erroneous apotheosis of the State), Protestant theology of law has not yet developed any concrete criteria to indicate under what pre-conditions and to what degree worldly legal structures could be taken over by the Church. This is particularly true on the whole question of pluralism.

Hans Dombois/*Heidelberg, West Germany*

The Basic Structure
of Church Law

One of the results of Vatican Council II is the need for a thorough-going revision of Canon Law. This new approach must be a reform because in principle the Church cannot and will not change the structures rooted in her foundation and tradition. But it must also be a new creation, because only now is there a binding teaching on the Church to which Canon Law must correspond and according to which the existing law must be changed where necessary.

The 1917 Code systematized and clarified the legal system as it developed in history, without, however, such an ecclesiology. Its method showed the positivist approach: it ordered the legal matter without linking it up with principles and without explicitly justifying it theologically. The same positivist approach is seen in the assumption that the formula of the Roman lawyer Caius for organizing all this material (persons—things—actions) does not affect the spirit and content of the law. The opposite is true. The Code was not only externally assimilated to the secular codes of the 19th century, but became unintentionally a creation of legal thought at that time.

Like any civil code the 1917 Code started by defining general notions and laid down the law for persons, since this law is necessarily, like any other, a matter between persons. But then it designated the clergy as the subjects of law whose duty it is to manage the objects of law, the "things" (*res*), above all the sacraments, in their divine ministry, and who are essentially the only ones called and enabled to do so. In this way the trustee-like and serving nature of the Church's offices is formally safeguarded throughout, but at the same time it introduces a subject-object pattern into the legal mentality. At the civil level, legal thought operates precisely in this opposition of (free or duty-bound) subjects and objects, particularly with regard to things over which these subjects exercise control. And so we have an unintentional assimilation of the Code to the spirit of the time. The main objects treated in this way are the sacraments, and yet it is not a law of sacraments. The Caius formula, borrowed from civil law, operates juridically like an institution. An institution exists detached from the persons who function as its officials, and is meant to benefit a particular set of persons. These persons have a subjective claim to the administration of the property of the establishment, insofar as they fulfill the conditions required. But as a subjective law this active law is not developed into a collegiate or membership law.

Because of its outward image, Canon Law is frequently interpreted as the law of a spiritual monarchy. It certainly contains elements of this character in an historically conditioned and politically absolute form. As established, it can be logically interpreted in law as an institution whose administrators have a perpetual right to self-preservation and the management of which is outside the control of those who benefit by the establishment. The stronger this institutional character, the more it displays an individualistic feature. The power is bestowed on the individual but he has no link with the others. In contrast with the spirit of Vatican Council II, the character of the Church as a community, *communo* and *koinonia*, is then referred to the realm of a mystical inner life and cut out of the realm of law. In no other historical form of Church organization are spirit and law so radically severed. They are only kept together by the demand of the faith to accept this tension and this opposition and to carry the burden of its harsh consequences. In truth, therefore, the problem does not lie in personal authority but precisely in the supra-personal objectivity of the aim of the institution, which is detached from the person.

The Evangelical observer is surprised to see how little the real Church and her work are recognized in law. The Catholic Church has taken upon herself the odium of a legal Church, both internally and externally. Her juridical interest is strictly limited to the legitimization of those empowered to act and to the plain normative fixing of the rights and duties of all her members. The actual legal content of her actions seems to fall outside her consideration.

However, as a result of Vatican Council II, the Church is now seen primarily and centrally as the People of God—in legal terms, as a covenant community. Thus those oppositions and separations fall away; there is no longer a separation between the inner and outer elements—i.e., between a legal Church and a mystical body, between those who are solely empowered to act in the Church and those who are only entitled to receive the benefits. Therefore, we must develop a new legal view of the Church and express her conduct in fitting juridical concepts. Here it is much easier to explain that basic ecclesiology in vivid and varied descriptions, as the Council did, than to express it in the binding and strict terms of a legal concept.

The idea of the People of God is, however, not merely a biblical reference to prove a theological statement or a full-blown theological thesis; it refers to the central event of salvation which can be interpreted legally and needs such an interpretation in order that Church law can be made to correspond to the nature and mission of the Church. Nor can we separate the legal notion of the People of God from that of the covenant with God. If the Council therefore understood the Church as the People of God, then the implied covenant structure must be legally worked out. The traditional saying *Ubi societas, ibi ius* ("Where the society is, there is the law") is then wrong if it means that the Church—which is as such, in the spiritual sense, beyond law

—can appropriate the forms of law in a secular (*innerweltlich*) sense. The Church is rather a legal bond and a legal community because God chose himself a people, entered into a covenant with them, and made them his own.

The fundamental legal concept on which the whole of Church law rests is therefore not the *societas* but the *foedus* (covenant). Modern exegesis of the New Testament has produced an abundance of fundamental legal statements about God's saving activity and the way they were applied in the apostolic Church. These must not be understood as symbolic images but as central to theology—e.g., covenant, testament, apostolate, heritage, property, adoption, witness. E. Käsemann's studies of *Sätze Heiligen Rechts im Neuen Testament* (*Tenets of Holy Law in the New Testament*) constitute a major contribution to this theme. But the recognition of these facts occurs everywhere and stands in need of a comprehensive explanation.

Thus the conclusion of a covenant is a procedure by which one party enters upon an active and lasting relationship with the other party. Equality between the partners is not essential to this notion. A covenant between unequal partners implies that one partner assumes the mastery, while the other accepts this and is given a place in this "dominion", but acquires at the same time a definite legal "status" in the structure of this dominion. That is why in the ancient liturgy of the early Church the baptized Christian stood upright while the catechumen knelt. Thus the covenant creates a situation where there is a certain condescendence, a waiving of rights. The higher party accepts a common legal bond with the lower party and takes this relationship as binding. This relationship cannot be adequately contained in normative categories, although obligations arise out of this legal concession. This is why a doctrine of natural law, which works with axiomatic imperatives, does not enter into this situation of life and law.

As President of the Papal Reform Commission, Cardinal Felici said at the International Congress of Canon Lawyers (Rome, May 1968) that the plan of the new Code would not be based on the Caius formula but on the teaching about the three functions of Christ. And so, for the first time, important theological statements have become the foundation of the Code.

Such a theologically founded division of the legal matter directly implies that the basis and definition of the Church's activity must be presented and defined in the light of a binding statement by the Church about herself. The connection of ecclesiology and Canon Law thus demands the formulation of a *Lex Fundamentalis Ecclesiae*. What it is possible and necessary to say here must fit in with the content and structure of the divine covenant and of the people of the covenant. This covenant has a twofold structure in three directions:

1. It comes *from* the new covenant with God (New Testament) once and for all concluded in the person of Jesus Christ, and is constantly renewed in the acceptance and incorporation of new generations and new people. This covenant is a continuing process of tradition—from tradition to tradition.

2. The conclusion of the covenant always means a selection from ("out of") the world, and leads to the building of its own community.

3. Once the covenant is granted and concluded, it gives the members a status *coram Deo* (in the presence of God), and at the same time obliges them to be active both ethically and in a missionary sense, in the expansion of God's kingdom.

As a result of these twofold personal structures, we can never speak ecclesiologically and juridically of the Church in terms of one single, closed concept, but always in terms of the form and description of a twofold, dual and plainly dialectic event. What happens in the Church is both forgiveness of sins *and* sanctification, detachment from the world *and* embodiment in a new existence, a present gathering *and* a missionary spreading out. This dual character can already be seen in the way Paul describes his call in the introduction to the epistle to the Romans. He speaks about being *aphorismenos*—i.e., selected, seized—but he also has the "grace and the office of an apostle"—that is, spiritual gifts and the institutional apostolate.

These statements are not identical but they belong together. The selection does not yet imply the gifts and powers, which are more than and something different from the selection. They are at least two clearly distinguished aspects—or, better, two acts that follow each other logically. In his sociology of law, Max Weber described such acts as status contracts, as procedures through which somebody is made to belong to somebody (*jemand jemandes wird*). Thus God establishes himself as Lord of his people, natural man becomes a son of God, and the Christian without a function becomes the holder of an authorized office. Legal theory can therefore make the transactions which occur in the New Testament and the consequent activities of the Church intelligible as legal actions that operate in a specific structure, as procedures of a "personalist institution". In contrast with the usual view, the institution is therefore not a static and fixed element but an historical and dynamic process by which concrete persons are taken out of their previous situation *and* incorporated in a new status which entails an appointment *to* something, a being related to.

If we start with the legal status of all Christians as members of the People of God, as a personalist legal community founded in baptism, we can then proceed with a reassessment of the co-ordination and cooperation of all the groups, associations and positions in the Church in detail. In this way the Church herself is not an "institution" outside, above, or detached from her members as she appears to be in the present law according to the interpretation I have given above. The Church is rather the place, the meeting point, where all those activities through which people are accepted into the covenant with God and are coordinated in view of this covenant. It is only in this theory of the Church as a personalist institution that the law of the sacraments comes into its own. The building up of the Church as the body of Christ continues uninterrupted in such activities. These are always dual (in the above sense) because they always link selection and purposeful coordination in one continuing process. A legal doctrine based on the theory of a personalist institution is therefore able to understand and explain the Church's sacramental activity in legal terms.

This also fits in with the teaching of Church government and makes for a better understanding of it. The "power of jurisdiction" and the "power of order" are not separate powers in view of separate tasks which operate side by side, without any connection, and whose relationship escapes all legal clarification. Just as in baptism, renunciation and exorcism (as detachment from the world) are linked with the positive elements in baptism as such, and just as at an ordination the selection "from" and the bestowal of a function in the actual ordination follow each other, so are the power of order and the power of jurisdiction logically bound up with each other. *Iurisdictio omnio est decisio de indicatione ordinationis* (Jurisdiction is based altogether on ordination).[1] Ordination covers all the sacramental actions which incorporate a person in the Church or give him a certain status in the Church. This new interpretation of the teaching of Church government disposes of many theoretical difficulties and doubts.[2] With the introduction into Canon Law of the doctrine of Christ's threefold function, the problem arises how this doctrine relates to the two powers of order and jurisdiction. For, if this doctrine has no connection with the two-powers structure, their interrelationship becomes an unsolvable problem, in theory and practice. Therefore I like the suggestion that the prophetic function refers to *all* men, inside and outside the Church, while the kingly function of jurisdiction is related to the priestly function of order, and both these powers operate exclusively inside the Church. This avoids confusion.

Without prejudicing the outcome of the controversial question about the origin of a special power of magisterium as the

---

[1] Cf. the detailed treatment given by H. Dombois, *Das Recht der Gnade. Oek. Kirchenrecht* I (Witten, 1961), ch. XIII, esp. pp. 836f.

[2] The Lutheran Church has taken over the so-called "old division", the teaching of the power of jurisdiction and of order, in art. XXVIII of its *Confessio Augustana, "De potestate episcoporum"*, although in somewhat narrower terms.

third kind of ecclesiastical power, I wholly agree with the view that ecclesiastical power can only be represented by the two powers of order and jurisdiction and that their factual relationship is best explained by the legal teaching on institutions. The question of the important doctrinal statements about the three functions (*munera*) is a different matter, since these functions are inextricably intertwined.

The ideas that came to the fore at Vatican Council II are not limited, however, to the internal structures of the Church. The Council gave a powerful stimulus to the missionary and ethical obligations of the Church and of Christianity. But this makes it necessary for Canon Law, starting afresh, to define in legal terms the relationship of the Church to the separated Churches and ecclesial communities, to non-Christians and the world community of mankind at large. If the Church relates to all these groups of persons, linked with her in various degrees of closeness, she must recognize their existence in their various degrees of relevance and determine the right and duty to cooperate and her relation to them in terms binding upon herself.

A basic orientation of Church law, placed at the beginning of the Code, must therefore embrace from the start the Church's own internal structures and her relation to her partners without. It must be placed in an ecumenical perspective. It should be conceived in such a way that, without prejudice to the irreplaceable qualities of the Church of Rome, it will also be as far as possible acceptable to non-Roman Christians. It must be a Code which starts from the concept of the People of God and which sees in this People as a whole the bearer of the three functions (*munera*) of Christ; this teaching will then find itself assured of wide support. Thus the teaching of the three functions is profoundly appreciated by the Calvinists and has been extensively developed by a canonical lawyer like Erik Wolf. It is accepted in Lutheran theology and may also be welcome to the Oriental Church. The Code can make use of the fact that an important amount of traditional Church law (e.g., baptism by heretics, prohibition of reordination, the building up of the Church in communities, synod law and many other matters) is shared by all, or at least all the great denominations, even today. The concept of a constitution for the Church which would begin by setting up a broad, yet binding, framework for the whole of Christianity, before it starts dealing with individual legal institutions, is something we have needed for centuries, and at the same time an opportunity which we cannot afford to ignore.

Church law can only be dealt with today in ecumenical terms. In its own situation, Protestantism has already begun to put the concepts of Church law in an ecumenical context, and Dietrich Pierson has provided a systematic treatment of this theme in his *Universalität und Partikularität der Kirche* (Munich, 1965). In all this the idea is not to even out the contrasts in a spirit of well-meant accommodation or to start with speculative presuppositions. The plurality of the traditions existing in Church law rather constitute a coherent whole, and the present problems show a common perspective. A reform of the Code clearly demands an elaboration of Latin and Oriental law in this plurality. Over and above that, it must aim at the possible unity of the Church. These problems must be solved on the basis of the whole tradition of Christianity and approached with new means in a forward-looking way.

Paul Winninger/*Strasbourg, France*

A Pastoral
Canon Law

I

THE PASTORAL PURPOSE OF THE LAW

When John XXIII announced the convocation of Vatican Council II, he said that it would be a *pastoral* Council. The expression became popular but lost some of its meaning because of the excessive and sometimes irritating use made of it. Yet the Church's concern, as expressed at the Council and as it will be formulated in the new Code, is clearly pastoral.

What does this mean? The word must be taken in its broadest sense, as practically synonymous with *mission:* "Go, teach and baptize. . . . Feed my sheep." These words of Christ show us two stages and two spheres of operation: evangelization or strictly missionary activity, outward-looking and concerned with non-believers at home or abroad, and inward-looking pastoral work, the care of the sheep in the fold, entrusted to their shepherds: teaching, worship and the building up of the People of God. We all know about the occasionally sharp tensions between these two purposes. These quarrels, spread out over articles and whole books, are rather painful. While it was necessary to shake Christianity out of a certain somnolence and to press for the urgency and no doubt the priority of the evangelization of non-believers, it would be wrong to neglect the worship and

51

the service of the faithful. That is why we must absolutely refuse to separate these two fields of pastoral activity, and in this refusal we can be sure of following the will of the Lord as authentically interpreted by the Council. The new Canon Law must be integrally pastoral, without separating the two aspects of the apostolic mission.

If it does this, it will be a great advance on the Code of 1917. For this Code, which is still with us, condensed ten centuries of Christian legislation into something coherent but rather detached from actuality. There is barely a trace of the present world, with its separation of Church and State, its spiritual pluralism, its industrial and urban civilization. The Code is still based on the system of benefices, and that means that it is still rooted in the *ancien régime*. That is why it is pastorally mediocre, from the internal point of view, where the faithful are concerned, and practically meaningless from the external point of view, with regard to the non-believers. When, after the works published by Godin-Daniel and Boulard, the pastoral renewal began in 1945 in France, and an attempt was made to put pastoral work on a comprehensive basis, it was curious to see that the defenders of the Code, so worried about parochial independence (conceived in terms of the old benefices), were opposed to these projects. There was a search for canonists obliging or subtle enough to prove that the Code could easily be interpreted in a way which authorized, or at least did not forbid, comprehensive pastoral work.[1] In fact, the Code was practically stillborn and out of date.

Hence the need and the difficulty of a new draft. It would be an illusion and once again an abortive operation if we aimed at a simple adaptation of the 1917 Code, with its existing framework and categories. We shall have to create something that is mainly new; we can no longer hark back to Gratian to extract and combine old formulae, but must start thinking constructively with the help of the two living sources of the law—namely, the Gospel and our own age—in the new light of the Council.

Do we have the courage and the ability to do this? The pres-

[1] Cf. *La Maison-Dieu* 57 (1959).

ent state of the Faculties and Institutes of Canon Law does not inspire much optimism. These schools and professors are more worried about erudition than about pastoral reflection and have turned Canon Law into a rather fossilized theological discipline. The gap is quite obvious: missionary research and experience owes practically nothing to the canonists. Will they change and cooperate with the *aggiornamento,* now that the Council is over? So far there is not much evidence of this. Yet the moment has come to redefine the real purpose of those institutions. This purpose is basically pastoral, even in the juridical sphere where this is not immediately evident. In sound Christian thought there is no room for an autonomous law: it does not exist. Even the most technical questions, such as those regarding powers and duties, dispensations, prohibitions and penalties, must refer to the Gospel, morality and the building up of the People of God. We must try to work out how we can and must live in order to "do the truth" (Jn. 3, 21), while taking great care not to substitute ourselves for that truth.

In order to achieve this, the Institute of Canon Law should broaden their horiizon and join the pastoral worker again, for he is the one they have to serve. Their program should therefore include the study of the actual conditions of the mission (religious sociology). Better still, they could be turned into Pastoral Institutes, not in view of the direct pastoral work at the concrete and local level of a diocese, for that is the business of the bishop and his council of priests, although even there the presence of the canonist would be desirable, but rather in view of some basic thinking about pastoral work, about the situation of the Church in our time, so that we can have some laws and institutions that are in harmony with this. At present this kind of research is broken up into three ill-coordinated branches of study: pastoral theology, religious sociology and Canon Law. Only by bringing them together into one basic approach can we hope for something really fruitful, at the level of what we are planning: a new Code.

II
SOME GUIDING PRINCIPLES

What would be the guiding principles for the drafting of a
Code that would be genuinely pastoral in intent? We could draw
up a complete list simply by deducing them from the texts of the
Council. I simply offer a few, rather obvious ones without any
pretense at being complete or methodical, since the limited
scope of this article does not allow greater leeway. The following
principles are simply derived from or corollaries of the basic
pastoral principle which embraces and implies them, and which
can be formulated in various ways, such as *Salus populi suprema
lex esto* ("Let the good of the people be the supreme law"), or
Sacramenta propter homines ("The sacraments are there for the
people") as long as we understand by this the Church as the
supreme sacrament which is meant to minister all of them.

1. *An Evangelical Law*

The Council insisted on the duty to refer and return to the
Gospel. Now, one can hardly say that the term "Gospel" fits in
easily with that of "code of law". It is true that the adjective
"evangelical" often emits a wholly unrealistic seraphic perfume,
when it ought to evoke the fine sense of balance embodied in
God incarnate. And so there are two ways of betraying the
Gospel.

First, by having too little of the Gospel, when the law introduces what Jesus threw out: vanities, the lust for power, privileges, etc.—and, as we know, in the Code there are sizable doses
of these ingredients which can only hamper the mission. "Show
me your man and I shall show you your God." The man, the
cleric as delineated by the Code, is occasionally not exactly an
example of evangelism. On certain points the civil codes and the
declarations of human rights have more in common with the
Gospel.

Second, by "overdoing" the Gospel. This is just as serious, although it is never mentioned. It happens when the law "improves" upon the Gospel and turns what is optional into an obligation, a counsel into a commandment, with a kind of pretense that we must be more Christian than Christ, just as some people are more royalist than the king. This false idealism is not evangelical, and it, too, obstructs the Christian mission. Such, for instance, is the status of the clergy in the Western Church, invented instead of taken from (*traditus*) the New Testament, hardened instead of supple, uniform instead of allowing for variety. It is not right to demand of the "episkopos" and the deacon any virtues that pretend to be of a nobler character than those mentioned by St. Paul (1 Tim. 3, 2-13), as if those of St. Paul were too common, good enough for antiquity, but far too ordinary for today. One can only hope that these virtues may flower, but also that by trying too hard to be like an angel one does not turn too quickly into an animal. The conciliar texts show a constant tendency toward something "too beautiful" which is not necessarily either good or true, a bias toward the superlative which is unknown to the New Testament, an expression of holiness which is sentimental rather than authentic, a monotonous celestial harmony which induces sleep and makes one lose touch with reality. This is not the Gospel. Such an ethereal Canon Law would simply bring about a divorce between the Church and that world in which she should be like a leaven.

2. A Realistic Law

First of all, vanities and silly things like the privileges of cardinals are not realistic. Paul VI has fortunately already begun to rectify this situation bit by bit. Nor is it realism to have laws which either cannot be or in fact are not applied. This is the greatest defect of any legislation. Yet the idealism of the Council comes close to steering in that direction. A too wide gap between the law and the facts is pastorally ruinous because one either lives in a hypocritical situation or quite simply outside the boundaries of real life.

As an illustration of a law that is not applied, there is ecclesiastical celibacy which is frequently unobserved in Latin America but to which ecclesiastical authority closes its eyes. This brings the Church into disrepute, and things will become worse with the cultural progress of the people. In such a case one should either face the facts and change the law or make the law work. We find laws among the various duties of the priest, particularly the parish priest, listed in the Code and amplified by the Council,[2] which cannot be put into practice as a whole today by a clergy that is already lacking in number and overburdened. One may say that this is true but that these texts point to an ideal and that in reality everybody tries to do what he can.

It is precisely this lack of realism which I protest. A duty is always an ideal, and to do what one can is often not enough. This duty should be set out in human terms and be within a man's capacity—that is, it must be credible and capable of being fulfilled reasonably with good will; in short, it must be possible. Then, indeed, a man will make an effort and rightly strive toward an ideal. But, faced with an excessive load, he loses hope or shrugs his shoulders and passes by. To so discourage priests is a pastoral catastrophe. Let the law therefore adopt the realism and humility of the Gospel: sufficient unto the day is the evil thereof, and don't let us add cubits to our stature.

3. A Coherent Law

By coherence I mean the logic which leads from the principles to their application. This is again a form of realism. It is a useful though somewhat painful exercise to read the documents of the Council—the *Constitution on the Church,* the *Decree on the Pastoral Office of Bishops in the Church,* the *Decree on the Ministry and Life of Priests* and the *Decree on the Church's Missionary Activity*—and then to reflect at the end of every section: This is the principle, the aim to pursue, but how do we set

---

[2] *Decree on the Pastoral Office of Bishops in the Church,* n. 30; *Decree on the Ministry and Life of Priests,* nn. 18-19.

about it in practice? What kind of institutions does the text imply? Where and how do we apply this? And one is left in a state of perplexity.

It was the Council's business to proclaim noble truths. The new Code is supposed to apply them. It will no doubt do so, albeit timidly, for it is a long way from saying something to doing it. But history proves that ultimately there is nothing so violent and effective as an idea, and many will no doubt be surprised at the institutional upheavals resulting from an obstinate scrutiny of the documents of the Council. There will be much insistence about being given the means with which to pursue the objectives laid down, since, like heads of State, the hierarchy is always tempted to lay down a policy beyond its means. And where the Church is concerned, the gap is as wide as infinity: to bring about the kingdom is beyond man's scope, for only God is able to do so.

And so we are left with the possible. Here the legislator has to provide the apostle with the means for his mission; otherwise he fails in his legislative function and contradicts himself. To give an example: "No Christian community, however, can be built up unless it has its basis and center in the celebration of the most holy eucharist." [3] Here we have a truth as solid as a dogma, whose application obviously requires the presence of a priest in every community. And here lies the first pastoral duty of the legislator. But he fails to do this, and the actual and most common image of the Church in vast regions is precisely that of communities that have neither priest nor eucharist and are in the process of disintegrating. Another example: "The power of the bishops is proper, ordinary and immediate. . . . The pastoral office . . . is entrusted to them completely. . . . [They will appoint] in each diocese a clergy sufficient in number and quality for the proper care of the People of God." [4] This constitu-

[3] *Decree on the Ministry and Life of Priests,* n. 6.
[4] *Constitution on the Church,* n. 27; *Decree on the Pastoral Office of Bishops in the Church,* n. 23.

tional truth of the Church demands a fulfillment and the end of the present incoherence where the papal power paralyzes that of the bishop in his primary duty, the pre-condition for missionary work—namely, the appointment of a sufficiently large number of priests. How can anyone be a bishop under those conditions?

4. *A Catholic Law*

Unity and catholicity, far from being synonymous, are opposites as characteristic features of the Church, and must find their balance in their complementary nature. The first missionary age, up until the 10th century, was catholic, respected the human values of the various civilizations and absorbed them in a remarkable process of symbiosis. Then confusion of catholicity with Western unity seems to have developed. After the discovery of the earth as a planet at the Renaissance, the second missionary wave showed an admirable courage, but the sense of Pentecost weakened and Christians unconsciously yielded to the Babel-like temptation of uniformity, a negation of catholicity. European rites were imposed on the lands of the new world. Missionary work had some success in the underdeveloped civilizations of Africa and America, but it failed in the higher civilization of Asia. China is an illustration of this catastrophe.

A third phase of missionary work, catholic like the first, dawned at Vatican Council II. The texts are clear enough but still have to be proved true. We are waiting for the new Code. Catholicity requires different codes, adapted to the customs and traditions of the various nations, linked with a common center which must ensure the unity of the constitutive institutions of the Church. There will have to be three levels in this legislation: the diocese (synodal statutes), the nation or a group of nations forming one cultural area, and the universal Church. The new element which is most necessary for pastoral progress lies at the second level. Episcopal conferences of regional synods must be given wide legislative powers, a broad autonomy, within communion with Rome. It is above all at this level that collegiality should operate. It is the only way in which we can build up catholicity, encourage ecumenism and make a new start with missionary work in non-Western countries.

5. *An Experimental Law*

We have to make contact again with real life, apart from sin, and not impose a system borrowed from past legislations or imagined out of the blue. In the present world of change, which is the "today" of God, the only hope of creating this link with real life lies in the humble courage to try things out and advancing by experiment. There are acute problems: vocation, priesthood, ecumenism, the parish, and others. We cannot solve them *a priori* or by referring to a past which itself started as an experiment but is now dead. A healthy pragmatism which preserves the immutable truth, but which cuts down things that have been wrongly absolutized and are the fruit of pseudo-traditions, will make it possible to fit the mission into the present world. We must therefore think in terms of codes at all the three levels in a state of continuous creation, for such is life.

6. *A Law Respecting the Hierarchy of Values*

The common good must override the particular interests of individuals. A priority scale of values helps to prevent the law from absolutizing everything, which leads to blockages. The most dramatic illustration of this today is the status of the clergy which has become an obstacle to the Christian mission instead of a means, and which is imposed on that mission instead of being subordinated to it. The same holds for the system of benefices: instead of being subordinated to pastoral work it has ended up by using pastoral work to its own advantage. It is feeding the shepherd instead of the flock. Hence the legal obstacles or hesitations when it comes to setting up an age limit, carving up dioceses or parishes that are much too vast, or removing the unworthy or inadequate from their office.

In all these cases the advantage of one individual, the office-holder, is allowed to override the good of the people with disastrous consequences for the people. The law seems to consecrate the ministry as a kind of personal property, and to confuse, more or less consciously, the indelible character of the sacrament with its ministry. It hardly dares even conceive of putting an end to this ministry, unless as a penalty involving loss of clerical rights. This is a mistake. Thus the personal character of the sacrament of orders has obliterated its exercise which is a social function. And so we have reversed the hierarchy of values and compromised pastoral work.

7. The Collegial Principle

The Christian term for this is "communal", and as practiced in reality it is called charity. This is not sentimentality, but a reasoned, willing and generous mutual understanding between several people, instead of domination by only one. In teaching, the ecclesial institution has always been defined in terms of community, college or synod. At every level, councils and hierarchical degrees were set up to assist the leader: pope, bishop or parish priest. But gradually, and particularly in the parishes, the leader ended up absorbing all the functions, and so we have developed a system of one-man shows. In a truly thoroughgoing pastoral reform the one man must be given a council and assistants with real responsibilities. And one hopes that in the future a parish priest will normally be assisted by a deacon and a lay council. Will this produce a flood of conflict situations? No, because the basic duty is to understand one another—that is, to prove love in actual fact, and such proof is irrefutable. Without this proof and by steering clear of it in a one-man show, Christianity is not credible and pastoral work is without value.

There is no point in prolonging this list of principles, which could easily be done by taking the main themes of the Council: service, collegiality, religious freedom, People of God (to be associated with pastoral work, especially in the appointment of the pastors), ecumenism (drafting laws that come as close as possible to the institutions of the other Churches). All these points meet in the pastoral principle. Every article of the new Code should be tested by reference to this principle and its implications.

III
THREE MAIN FIELDS REQUIRING NEW LEGISLATION

The evangelization of non-believers and the pastoral service of the faithful particularly require new legislation for the ministry, the benefice system and the community.

1. *The Ministry*

There is no pastoral work without pastors. Now there is no lack of bishops. But it does not make sense to see the number of bishops increase while the number of priests goes down. Whatever people say or do, pastoral work will decline under these conditions. Most countries already suffer from severe pastoral pressures which painfully contradict the documents of the Council. Instead of instituting the ministry, palliatives are used that threaten to throw everything into confusion; lay people, men and women, are made to distribute communion, to preach, and to supervise the community. Instead of bringing in reforms that fit in with theology and tradition, innovations are introduced which go against theology and tradition.

Every modern society marks off the scope and size of its structures and boundaries (boroughs, districts, etc.). It then sets up the number of necessary cadres (in administration, teaching, justice, health, etc.). Only the Church, which believes herself to be the perfect society, refuses to do so. Thus authority fails in its first duty and seems to be incapable of stopping the breakdown of the Church when it should be building her up. Turning away from the end, we are marching backward to a mission without missionaries and a pastoral activity without pastors. The number of priests diminishes because the statute of the clergy no longer fits into our present society: it is a statute based on benefices of an antiquated "Christendom" and harks back to the *ancien régime*. Just as the reform of the liturgy was impossible without getting rid of the obstacle of the Latin language, so we cannot recruit enough priests without eliminating the bottleneck of their present status. Not only has this status little in common with the principles mentioned above, but experience clearly shows its inadequacy.

There are two specific points, pastorally very important but only vaguely referred to by the Council, which must be mentioned. Severe age limits should be imposed throughout: the minimum age for the priest should be raised to thirty, and retirement should not be postponed beyond seventy. Lay members of parochial councils should be made liable to the same retirement limit; failure to do so has paralyzed the work of some of these councils. The second point concerns the curates, those "minors" among the clergy who constitute the first rung on the ladder of the ecclesiastical career (cf. my article, "Les villes aux mains des vicaires," in *Rev. de Droit canonique,* March 1958). When we have raised the age for ordination, suppressed the system of benefices, developed priestly communities, set up a comprehensive pattern of pastoral work and accepted the priority of the urban apostolate, the "curate" category should disappear altogether in normal circumstances.

2. The "Benefice"

The Council has eliminated this term and replaced it by "service", which is excellent. But the priest still has to live. There is no mention of the problem of subsistence and money, which is overdoing pastoral modesty. It was only later on that the question was tackled in nn. 20-21 of the *Decree on the Ministry and Life of Priests.* But what should be done? We have to find modern solutions to this important problem and insert them in the codes at all three levels. For over 1,000 years the life of the Church has been dominated by the system of benefices, which has affected all the facets and activities of the Church, particularly the organization of pastoral work. This regime has now more or less vanished from the modern scene.

Where then do we find the resources to provide bishop and

priests with a livelihood, to keep the various activities going, and to maintain old buildings or start new ones? The main point is the salary of the clergy. The least objectionable solution is payment by the State on the basis of a concordat, but this will no doubt become the exception in the future. Elsewhere, and that means in the greater part of the Christian world, there are ingenious practices where resources, reluctantly turned over, are derived from various collections, personal effects, donations, various forms of begging, the sale of candles, medals and blessings, fees for the signing of forms, stole fees which are a bargaining-in-disguise of sacraments and ceremonies, and, lastly, those Mass stipends, talk of which resounded in the conciliar corridors. This is really no longer possible. This dredging for money repels modern man who refuses two solutions which can be combined: to live supported by the Community, and to live by the labor of one's own hands. The new Code would do well to look there for a definition of the various possibilities, in conformity with the principles set out above and after discussing with the Christian people, leaving room for experiences other than the present situation which is no longer viable.

3. *The Community*

The minister and his benefice give us in fact the definition of the parish, the basic pastoral structure. By instituting priests and deacons in sufficient number and assuring their livelihood by a non-beneficial income, we arrive at a new definition of the cadre of the ministry and of new forms of community: that is the essential project of pastoral work. The Council did not make much progress in this direction. It frequently alluded to the dispersed and distant communities in the rural regions of Africa and Latin America, but not to the massive urbanization of this century. The parish, particularly in the cities, has become discredited because it is too vast, closed-in and out of touch with man's working life and his leisure. This territorial structure remains irreplaceable and more effective than any other, on condition that benefice is changed into service, which means: cutting it up into small units of human size, an end to the one-man show, integration into a comprehensive system, and a service by priests equally active and equally paid (no more curates).

In addition to parishes we could have other communities, based not on territorial boundaries but on "personal" or shared interests. Many are enthusiastic about this, and let us hope it is not an illusion. If these communities are given legal status, they should be oriented toward, or even subordinated to, the parishes, particularly by appointing the same pastors to both in order to avoid rivalries and, above all, a kind of Christian "class" distinction. The territorial parish has the essential advantage of promoting brotherhood among members regardless of age, sex, wealth, social rank, education and personal opinions.

But the pastoral problem cannot be limited to the parish; on this point we have been having discussions for twenty years, apparently without reaching any definite conclusions. The real problem lies in the *local church,* located in a main center of which the rural communities are simply outcrops. This was the ancient structure of the Church, and present urbanization seems to impose it again. On this point the canonist might absorb and try to convert into institutions the ideas contained in the admirable study of J. Comblin in *Theologie de la ville* (Paris, 1968).

One can then pass from the reorganization of the parish to that of dioceses, so very unequal and badly marked off. This problem is most urgent in Italy where the problem has been dragging its feet for forty years, ever since the Lateran agreement was signed in 1929.

The aim of missionary and pastoral activity is to build up the local Church by creating these Christian communities. It can only make progress when, with the help of the local Christians, the conditions already mentioned are realized, and among these the following three are the most important:

(a) to define the size of the basic eucharistic community by reducing it to the human scale;

(b) to institute ministers (priests and deacons) to whom

each community is strictly entitled and without whom it will perish;

(c) to solve in a modern and honest way the problem of the ministers' livelihood.

These are the indispensable conditions for any pastoral legislation of the future.

José Setién/*Vitoria, Spain*

Tensions in the Church

I

The Fact of Tensions in the Church

The historical fact of tension in the Church has to be our starting point. This will avoid a formalistic, juridical approach with its corresponding neglect of any attempt at drawing conclusions.

The existence of tensions is a many-sided phenomenon, which means it cannot be approached from a pre-conceived idea. Sometimes it appears as no more than the exercise of a legitimate freedom, on an individual or collective plane, within the bounds of legally recognized freedom of action; at other times there are the germs of formal disobedience, or at least actions contrary to the dictates of established laws.

The manifestations of tensions take different forms in different countries, varying with the nature of the country and its particular brand of ecclesial problems. Relations between the civil power and the Church undoubtedly have the same sort of influence as conflicts of interests and the taking up of positions within the Church. In one place there might be a group of students for the priesthood taking sides with colleagues who have been rejected and threatening a mass walkout; in another, there might be abstention from lectures as a weapon to introduce changes in the teaching staff or ideological approach of the establishment, or sit-ins by priests or lay people in churches or other ecclesiastical centers, or a secret priests' association laying down its own code of action, often different from the official one. The faithful can apply pressure by refusing to fulfill their Sunday obligation.

II

NEED FOR A THEOLOGICAL-AXIOLOGICAL CLARIFICATION

Theological criteria are essential if one is to be able to distinguish between acceptable and unacceptable tensions, not to mention being able to pose the question whether any form of tension in the Church is acceptable. What one has to find out is whether tensions can be integrated into a policy which seeks the well-being of the Church or not. This is a relatively new question, at least to the extent that tensions are now being considered not merely as one more element of the life of the Church, but also as a principle of progress within her which, to a certain extent at least, should therefore be encouraged. The theological criteria are to be found, it would seem, in reflection on unity and freedom in the Church.

1. *The Defense of Unity*

The unity of the Church is concerned with both vertical relationships within the community—obedience of subjects to authorities—and horizontal relationships between members of the ecclesial body—what for want of a better term one might call community cohesion. In the vertical relationships, tensions spring from the resistance offered by individuals or groups to the will of a superior. They are a confrontation with authority, acceptance of which has to be considered one of the basic, integrating factors in the well-being of the community. The opposition can take a stand on legal grounds, in which case obedience to the law is not called into question, or it can show itself in illegal actions, in which case there is at least an external or material break with obedience.

If authority, in accordance with its original mission, is a body that guides, stimulates, promotes, orders, foresees, plans and fixes objectives for action, then resistance to it would seem, at first sight at least, to be a threat to the common good. This holds true particularly for a community interested not only in the external order of justice, but in the internal assent of faith and intellectual discipline as well.

But unity would also be broken by tensions within the body of the Church not involving authority. There would be a direct break in community, analogous to that produced in the body politic by competing groups and political parties, trade unions and other such organizations when they engage in sterile disputes between collective egoisms instead of cooperating in the communal task of building up the common good. In such cases confrontation wastes the resources of the country.

There is more to it in the Church than this sociological aspect, since the theological view of the problem also has to be considered. It is the Church as a communion, signified and realized by the eucharistic celebration, that would be fragmented, so bringing about the paradox, real or apparent, that all partake of the one sacramental body while belonging to groups and factions that destroy external unity. The tendency would then be for those who belong to a separated group to celebrate their own eucharist, apart from the rest of the Church.

2. *The Defense of Freedom*

Obedience and unity are not the only considerations; the Church is also a community in which freedom has a part to play. She is a community of free men, enjoying not only the personal liberty implied by freedom from the bondage of sin, but also the collective freedom supposed by the fact that social relationships are inspired by the ideal of liberty.

Yet social freedom is inseparable from a juridical recognition of freedoms; it is only real when there are recognized degrees of autonomy and self-determination and these produce individual and collective rights to freedom which are at least different and often conflicting.

If situations of tension can be defined as those in which the pursuit of different interests leads to collective confrontations, then one is forced to conclude that tension is a spontaneous derivation from the affirmation of liberty. This is why, in affirming or denying the legitimacy of a situation of tension, there is one basic value of the Christian's social existence within the ecclesial community that has to be taken into account: liberty itself.

The defense of freedom in the Church has to be something more than a defensive reaction against totalitarian abuses; it has to be seen as an integrating element in an ecclesial-social climate in which the creative capacity of each sector can come to the fore. The principle of subsidiarity holds good in the Church as well as in the State, though not in quite the same way. Society as well as authority has to have a care for the well-being of the Church, and for this it needs freedom of expression and of action.

This is a secular consideration, but it holds good for the Church to the degree that the laws governing the way men live together in society are bound to apply to a society such as the Church. A strictly religious approach would lead to the same conclusion, bearing in mind that the gifts of the Spirit, given for the *edificatio*—building up—of the People of God, take root in the whole body of the Church, with a spontaneity that escapes and surpasses the gifts handed down through exclusively hierarchical channels. Charisms are not given for the overthrow of the right order established or sanctioned by authority, but they do require a certain measure of freedom. Thus it would seem logical to conclude that once the idea of freedom is admitted, tensions will ineluctably follow, and that behind the tensions there will be not only a selfish or divisive spirit but also the spirit of unity itself.

Therefore tensions have to be seen as intimately linked to the development of the life of the Church community, rooted as this is in the contributions brought by natural human gifts and by the contribution brought by the Spirit—difficult to tie down and liable to lead the Church along uncharted courses. For the Church to adapt to the continual flux of historical situations, and to have grasped these situations in the first place, requires a social mobility that will overcome stagnation and social sclerosis. Community freedom and its concomitant effect, the existence of tension, have to be at the service of this social mobility.

III
EVALUATING THE EXISTENCE OF TENSIONS

Starting from a basic notion of what constitutes the common good of the Church, which must provide the criterion of what is socially beneficial or harmful, we now have to decide whether tensions act against this common good or for it. By the common good of the Church I understand that social situation of the ecclesial community which provides the necessary conditions for the individual Christian to accomplish his own religious perfection and for the community in general to carry out its task of evangelization and sanctification.

Taking the personalist values inherent in any society into account in the Church shows that the common good can be produced not only through obedience (given the proper exercise of authority), but also through individual and collective creativity in the exercise of freedom. This double perspective, of obedience and freedom, is not contradictory but complementary. Neither element of the common good has to be suppressed, but both must be integrated in a correct balance, in which the determinant historical circumstances of any given situation will play a crucial role.

Thus the oft-heard affirmation that tensions can only be tolerated in the measure that they contribute to the common good has to be understood correctly. It has in itself no more force than the parallel affirmation that could be made: that authority can only be tolerated in the measure that it shows itself to be compatible with the common good. Neither tensions, which are the fruit of freedom, nor obedience, which is the fruit of respect for authority, are evils to avoid, but goods to be conjoined in the higher value of the common good. But saying this is hardly a solution to the problem of social unity, and it would be childish to suppose that it was. Ideological resistance to authority, in the extreme case, will lead to heresy or near-heresy; disciplinary resistance stretched to the limit will end in schism; internal divisions waste apostolic forces and lead to scandals in the community.

On the doctrinal plane, the solution has to come from an acceptance of different levels of unity, and not every lack of it implies the loss of the theological value of unity. It can even be said that a certain social pluralism is compatible with the constitutive unity of the Church, and, more than that, is necessary if the Church is to carry out her mission.

On the pastoral plane, the solution cannot be so clear-cut. Differing degrees of maturity in different communities mean that some are more capable of withstanding tensions without scandal than others, and this fact has to be seen as an objective criterion of the common good, though not the only one, because other factors are just as important: desire for reform, institutional change, or any development, short- or long-term, which will be for the overall benefit of the People of God. And the more heavily the institution is weighted against change, the stronger the tensions to force it into change have to be. Of course tensions bring the risk of disagreements, of ideological and disciplinary crises, but where they are lacking, there will be a failure to adapt, social petrification, and, in the long run, loss of effectiveness for the Church.

Seen in this way, the existence of tensions has to be seen in a positive light, to the extent that it is kept within bounds. Fixing these bounds—the institutionalization of tensions—will be an important task for the juridical arm, without this being the whole answer to the problem. This is a question of social freedom, and so a socio-cultural question which must take the religious character of the ecclesial community into account. Education in the use of freedom and democracy, in the Church as elsewhere, requires interiorization of motives for action to give due weight to the repercussions that decisions once taken will have on the common good.

If the institutionalization of tensions through the juridical arm is to act as keeper of the tension level within certain limits, set by consideration of the common good of the Church, this does not mean that the law is being elevated to the position of a supreme principle in the life of the Church—juridical positivism. (I shall have something to say at the end of this article on the present balance between tension and the law.) The fact that any juridical consideration of the problem has to be preceded by a theological one shows that the limits set to tensions have to come from objective ecclesial values, which take precedence over any attempt at juridical ordering. Otherwise, the institutionalization of tensions would become a purely arbitrary affair and would inevitably, through the dynamic of history, suffer fragmentation and relegation to the margins of the actual course of events.

When we go on to analyze the ecclesial goods that are the object of tensions and also the cause of ecclesial communion in faith and discipline, we shall see that it is these goods that have to determine the limits beyond which tensions cannot be allowed to trespass, since doing so would amount to multiplying Churches. This is admissible when Churches are considered as separate sociological entities, but must not reach the point of breaking up a Church considered as the basic unity of a single social group, the sign of its inner unity in Christ. But such a limit is not a matter of "rules" or "laws", but of living requirements for the building up of a communion.

One could perhaps talk of a sort of constitutional law, or basic ecclesial order, which tensions, at the very least, have to leave intact. But it seems inaccurate and even dangerous to do so, for one cannot ignore the fact that the historic embodiment of the constitution is also subject to revision, and that tensions are themselves one of the most effective agents for ensuring that this revision will be made. Without pushing the political parallel too far, one can say that just as the constitutions of nations evolve, so the historical order of the ecclesial community has to change.

The real difficulty is in deciding what is the basic order that has to be left intact, come what may. The solution will have to be found through a clarification of what the Church has to be in the divine plan, just as in the political order the divine will for society has to determine the limits within which human creativity has to operate in history. Such limits will be entitative in the first place, and later ethico-juridical. But to attempt to determine this brings one up against the well-known difficulties attached to any attempt at fixing the limits of this *ius naturale* within which the *ius humanum* is built up and determined.

Something similar happens when one tries to establish the divine basis of the ecclesial order. If for simplicity's sake we talk of a *ius divinum* in the Church, which would fix the lines of her standard evolution, we cannot ignore the way historical evolution itself obliges the Church to face up to situations which, once their consequences are accepted, produce a fuller realization of what the divine plan for the Church is, of what we mean by this *ius divinum*. Thus we find ourselves in the thick of a purely theological problematic which underlies any juridical considerations. But a solution to the problem cannot come from anything other than an acceptance of the fact that the very discovery of what is theologically basic has to come from a dynamic of tension, in which tension comes to affect the very essence of what living and being in the Church means. In such a situation, the risk of relativism and of breaking with what is permanent and handed down would be unavoidable if there were no "definitory" principle of transcendence within the ecclesial community itself, no principle of unity in authority, which means in the institution. Obviously, this view can affect the credibility of a Church which assumes these "definitory" powers to itself, but this is a question of faith. Believing in Christ within a particular ecclesial community is something more than just believing in a place or a sociological framework for faith; it must enter into the very definition of what one understands by believing.

Finally, the theological criterion is not the only one. There is also an historical-prudential one: the more maturely a community is able to cope with tense confrontations within itself, the more sensitive its members will be to the imperatives and practical requirements of the common good. Conversely, the more education and firmness in faith help to uncover the historical-relative nature of so many forms of life and action in the Church, the easier becomes the assimilation of the confrontations proper to tensions which seek to transcend outworn forms of life in the Church. This is why any tension-producing actions must be inspired by a great love for the Church, not by resentment or bitterness.

IV
ECCLESIAL GOODS AS THE OBJECT OF TENSIONS

Before embarking on the subject of the institutionalization of ecclesial tensions, it seems necessary to determine, in a general way, what the ecclesial goods are that can be the object of enriching tensions. Since the Gospel is a message that has to be passed on, a *depositum fidei,* the saving truth itself, possessed and communicated by the Church, will become an object of tension, along with immediate and practical social concerns, the tasks and objections of ecclesiastical "politics" in pursuit of the common good, or, if one prefers the term, discipline.

1. Faith and Doctrine

Revealed truth itself is a focus for imperfectly harmonious interests and positions. This should not be seen as putting the unity of Catholic faith in danger, or as seeking to give a relative character to revealed truth through a permanent process of historical adaptation. The magisterium of the Church is living and the truth it has to teach is historical. These two realities necessitate a permanent adaptation of the truth to current needs and historical situations, if the truth is to be kept sufficiently illuminating and saving. The Gospel truth does not exist as a function of itself, but as a function of the men in their historical situation whom it is to save. Also, the truth of the Church is the object of a continuous search.

The historicity of the message and the quest for truth, as is easily understandable, will give rise to tensions between tradition and innovation. The danger of making historical trappings, transient by nature, into a permanent and unchanging reality, and the converse danger of letting what the Church has to keep forever flow along on the tide of history, are bound to produce divergent and conflicting attitudes. One pole of the tension will always be the official magisterium, charged with examining and adjudicating; the other will come from the respect due to freedom of conscience in adhesion to the faith. And with freedom of conscience goes the exercise of the prophetic function, in private and public witness to personal faith, and also in the continual search for what adaptation to life requires in the way of innovation in the transmission of the message itself.

Doctrinal tension does not arise only between the magisterium and the community; it also arises between different sections in the community from which the authorities can, in principle, remain aloof. Integrists and progressives put forward views whose repercussions will affect the future well-being of the Church, without either party thinking of cutting itself off from the one Church.

2. Regime and Discipline

Tension can originate in purely ecclesial factors, such as differing approaches to the pastoral question, or differing estimations of the risk inherent in any choice of system of government. Or it can be produced by extra-ecclesial factors, such as sociopolitical affairs, which can give rise to differing behavior and attitudes in particular situations—questions of the temporality of apostolic associations, for example, or the exercise of prophetic denunciation of injustice, or assessment of benefits derived from collaboration with particular social or political groups.

Whether one opts for prudence or daring, the security of the already held position or the risk inherent in the conquest of new ones, the decisions of the authorities—and whatever seems to be an effective means, from some particular point of view, of putting pressure on these decisions—will alway be influenced by interpretations of the signs of the times and their repercussions on the life of the Church. There are, of course, pressure groups inside the Church as there are outside her, and other groups trying to counter them by similar means. The fact that all these groups or associations in the body of the Church claim to be working for the glory of God and service of the Church does not prevent them from making their own interests coincide with those of God. Even if they end by coming together for the good of the Church, opposing camps initially divide the community and, to a certain extent, bring it into confrontation with itself.

V
THE INSTITUTIONALIZATION OF TENSIONS

1. *Meaning*

Institutionalizing means something more than juridical ordering; it adds the idea of a public step, of the area of public rights of the individual, which must apply to both individuals and groups within the ecclesiastical framework.

Tension can be said to be institutionalized when rights are assigned to different members of the community, thereby guaranteeing them a sphere of competence and action, by virtue of the juridical protection implied in the assignation of rights. This permits the community to utilize its creative forces within the limits of the higher imperative of the common good. When different conceptions or spheres of interest confront each other in the exercise of individual or collective rights, then tension arises. But tension presupposes life and a lively interest in the life and growth of the Church; it is a sign of social riches and the communal dynamism that one expects from young communities.

2. Objective

Institutional ordering has to keep tensions within certain limits, keeping them consonant with the common good and preventing them from degenerating into destructive and anarchic struggles. But this is only the negative aspect of its task: it presupposes the positive side—the defense of the dynamic of society that makes tensions possible. A further consideration of this point is needed:

(a) *Affirmation of the Poles of Tensions.* Tension is always relative, and in a way dialectical; without opposing poles, it cannot exist. The law has to create margins for action that have to be respected; the institution affirms postions. It makes the play of tensions possible.

(b) *Guaranteeing the Goods of the Community.* The common good requires that the objective goods by whose possession the members of the community are enriched should be left intact. The easier it is to harm the community's goods, the more sensitive the community has to be to the way tensions and juridical ordering are worked out.

(c) *Higher Authorities.* Conflicts arising from tensions have to remain open to the possibility of a solution by recourse to a higher authority. This in its turn has to be impartial and to have pastoral vision and, above all, faith in the dynamic of society. It has to avoid falling into the routine of supporting the safer and less risky course; it has to postpone definite verdicts as far as possible and as far as is necessary to preserve salutary tensions.

(d *Clarification of Tensions.* A too narrow or limiting concept of the play of tensions can easily cause tension to overstep legal channels or operate on their fringe, clandestinely if need be. Thus there is need for great prudence on the part of authority to prevent the "necessity" of working out problems on the

fringe of the establishment in this way. It is better for tensions
to show themselves where they exist than to subsist unappreciated
by authorities in ignorance of the deep and true feelings of the
community.

(e) *The Defense of Authority*. If authority is to be able to
carry out its task of guiding and integrating, it has itself to
remain, as far as possible, on the sidelines of social tensions in
the Church. The highest authority has to leave more play to
lower structures; authority will then more easily be a sign of
unity, more easily remain sacred, demean itself less and be
accepted more.

(f) *Tension and Law*. The law has to stand above tensions;
the common good has to judge the law. Tension will occasionally
struggle against the law itself, And it is a valid question whether
progress will not sometimes demand actions against the law,
or—and this comes to the same thing—whether it would be
permissible to introduce disobedience as a method of progress
in the Church. This is to introduce the theme of revolution into
the Church—illegal activity as a means of introducing social
justice. This is not directly the subject of this article, but it could
not be passed over completely. While leaving the question open
for later studies, it is clear that its solution would have to be sought
in a deepening understanding of what is meant by a just and
useful law, through a historical-dynamic approach which would
take account of the necessary evolution both of social facts and
of the law. In other words, one cannot admit revolutionary
tension which acts against the established legal order as long as
this is considered objectively valid.

But while leaving open the possibility of acting against the law
in order to achieve what is right for the Church, one has to indicate some objective principles that will avoid a descent into the
arbitrariness of purely subjective judgment. Tensions operating
against the law will be of little use if they lead to the opposite
extreme of sanctioning any innovation merely because some subjective judgment elevates it into a requirement for the common

good. These objective principles will have to be derived from a study of the following three factors:

(a) *Openness to the Future*. We need a vision of the Church that recognizes the historical nature of her mission and her corresponding changeability. It is not enough for this to be recognized on the purely theoretical level; it has to be translated into a way that the ecclesiastical "apparatus" functions, with channels of communication open between all the different strata that make up the Church.

It should not be forgotten, however, that there are different rhythms of evolution and adaptation. The important thing is that the machine should work, even if this means authority deciding how fast the engine should run. And one should beware of false prophets, who love seeing into the future. Openness to the future should not be confused with foreseeing what is going to happen tomorrow; it is rather a *present* perception of the line of evolution that must be found, knowing that the future will bring changes even without being able to state what they will be.

(b) *The Conflict Between Rule and the Common Good*. The discovery and affirmation of this conflict has to start from a personalist conception of what constitutes the common good. Avoiding the selfish individualism of making society a function of the individual, one must affirm that social goods exist as a function of each person. This basic intuition has not been alien to the juridical ordering of the Church; there is the inner law of conscience, a good instrument for the defense of personal integrity against the "common interests" defended by the law. Nevertheless, there is room to think that the full consequences of the principle have not been drawn; if it can be said that it is the common good that suffers when any member of the community suffers by reason of the malfunctioning of the community, much will need to be changed if we are really to bring about the common good.

(c) *Certainty Based on the Proper Guarantees*. This is the crux of the question. For who is to decide when there exists a

conflict between rule and common good? The individual conscience cannot be an adequate criterion. There has to be recourse
to a sort of ecclesial *sensus communis,*in which the feeling of the
community will be made present. The solution to crises brought
about by evolution cannot come from the reiteration of opinions
closed to discussion, with the inevitable consequence of forcing the
opposing opinion into a radical stance. As the principle of communion with the Church comes to depend on fewer guarantees
offered by the juridical rule for acceptance, so the search for
other criteria of communion has to become more minute, and the
transcending of closed and isolated postions more determined. It
must be recognized, at this point, that neither theological nor
canonical studies have gone far enough in these questions.

Pedro Lombardía/*Pamplona, Spain*

The Fundamental Rights of the Faithful

That the fundamental rights of the faithful within the ecclesial community should be proclaimed in terms of canonical norms with, as it were, constitutional force, and that they should be protected by the entire complex of the Church's juridical system, is a natural consequence of the teaching of Vatican II concerning the dignity of those who are pilgrim members of the People of God. It seems reasonable, therefore, to hope that the proclamation of these rights should be one of the tasks of the forthcoming fundamental law of the Church[1] and that their protection should constitute one of the determining criteria of the current revision of Canon Law.[2]

However, this legislative task is not without difficulty, given that canonical research on the subject is so sparse and of such recent date that the only two monographs dealing with the fundamental rights of the faithful that seem to me of any real value have not been published at the time of this article's composi-

[1] I have dealt with this question in *Una legge fondamentale per la Chiesa* (Firenze, 1969), which will cover the matters dealt with by the 1967 Synod of Bishops.

[2] Cf. *Principia quae Codicis Iuris Canonici recognitionem dirigant*, n. 6, submitted for examination to the Synod of Bishops.

tion,[3] and that there exist in the Code of Canon Law practically
no relevant precedents.

I
THE FOUNDATION OF SUCH RIGHTS

The notion of fundamental rights presupposes an egalitarian
vision of all those who belong to the Church; on no other basis
could such rights be of universal application. Understood in this
sense, they have to be seen in connection with the *radical equality* that derives from the common condition of all the faithful,
that condition which is prior to any form of inequality based on
the principle of *variety* of *function*.[4] In other words, these fundamental rights are those belonging to all members of the faithful,
simply in virtue of their being such, simply by reason of their
status within the Church—that is, by reason of their dignity and
liberty as children of God.[5]

The title of "faithful" belongs to that man who has given an
affirmative answer to that divine *convocatio* (summons) which
is the Church. The call of God in the Church is directed to all
men without exception. The Church is for men and is built up by
men; that is why the subject of this article is intimately connected
with the so-called "rights of man". These have been the object
of philosophic reflection from the most widely varying points of
view and of numerous declarations of positive law, both in the
constitutional norms of various countries and in texts of an international character. But given that these "rights of man" provide us with a preliminary approximation to our theme, they still
stand in need of a much more precise critical definition; the vari-

---

[3] Cf. A. del Portillo, *Fieles y laicos en la Iglesia; Bases de sus respec-
tivos estatutos jurídicos,* and P. J. Viladrich, *Teoría de los derechos fun-
damentales del fiel; Presupuestos críticos.* Both of these books are to be
published this year, and I am grateful to the authors for allowing me to
use their original manuscripts.

[4] *Constitution on the Church,* n. 32.

[5] *Ibid.,* n. 9.

ous possible anthropologies can and in fact do imply very different solutions to the problem of human rights, and for that reason
the use of the notion of human rights as a means to solving the
problem of the fundamental rights of the faithful demands an
initial and evangelically based value-judgment on the anthropology taken as one's point of departure.

All this constitutes a question on its own, one that is still
open, given that the possibility of further progress can never be
excluded, but one concerning which nonetheless we already have
sufficient material, including authentic declaration by the critical
magisterium of the Church, that can be condensed into formulations of positive law. The so-called "social doctrine" of the
Church, particularly significant sources of which are the teaching
of the Roman pontiffs and certain documents of Vatican II (above
all the *Constitution on the Church in the Modern World* and the
Declaration of Religious Freedom), has taken a positive attitude
to that modern current of thought in favor of the rights of man
and seeks to bring it into harmony with Christian anthropology.
John XXIII's encyclical *Pacem in terris* proposes, among many
things, a list of rights that should be considered fundamental to
man. This teaching which implies the taking of a definite position
with regard to the foundation, nature, characteristics and juridico-
political function of fundamental rights, is applicable in its essen-
tials to the faithful, inasmuch as they are human persons within
the ecclesial community. That being so, it seems imperative—as
I have already pointed out on another occasion—to eliminate the
present discrepancy between what the magisterium demands in
this field from states, international organizations, etc. and what
the Church achieves in the juridical ordering of her own affairs.
It is a matter of urgency that the Church should authenticate her
social teaching by the witness of a vigorous defense of the rights
of man within the ecclesial community, taken here in the sense
of a juridically organized society. In this connection a great deal of
significance should be attached to the speech of Paul VI in which

6 "El Derecho en el actual momento de la vida de la Iglesia," in
Palabra 33 (May, 1968), pp. 8-12.

he related the revision of Canon Law to the celebration of the 20th anniversary of the Declaration of the Rights of Man of December 10, 1948.[7]

But to get to the heart of the riches contained in the theme of fundamental rights within the Church, it is not enough simply to consider the faithful as human persons. Over and above that, one must take into account the fact of their elevation to the super-natural order by baptism if one is to grasp the full ontological and sacramental scope alike of that in which these rights are grounded and of their relation with the mystery of the Church. Viladrich, surveying from this angle the teaching of Vatican II, observes that "the assertion of fundamental rights is, from a material point of view, the making subjectively explicit of certain aspects of the foundational will of Christ that are implicit in the ontological-sacramental condition of the faithful; these explicita-tions have reference on the one hand to spheres of autonomy (divine sonship) and on the other to spheres of activity (the universal priesthood). Formally these subjective principles of divine law constitute primary juridical notions".

II
THE CATALOGING OF FUNDAMENTAL RIGHTS

The texts of Vatican II, especially chapters 2 and 4 of the *Constitution on the Church,* provide us with extremely valuable doctrinal foundations for a positive solution of the problem of the existence of fundamental rights within the ecclesial community, foundations on which the very notion of these rights can be firmly set and which enable us to relate them with the mystery of the Church. However, as was to be expected, given the nature of its documents, this Council did not provide an exhaustive list of the fundamental rights of the faithful, even though cer-

[7] *Allocutio disciplinarum Iuris Canonici cultoribus qui interfuerunt coetui ex omnibus nationibus* (May 25, 1968).

tain individual ones were outlined with remarkable clarity;[8] much less could the Council provide solutions to all the problems of Canon Law relative to the protection of those rights by positive ecclesiastical law.

Seen from this angle, the question has to be posed in relation with the project of a *fundamental law of the Church,* conceived as the foundational legal text of constitutional Canon Law. Above all else the declaration of the fundamental rights of the faithful is one of the matters impossible to omit from that fundamental law, and to that end we have to solve the problem of listing them. Is it possible to make a concrete affirmation of the *number and character* of the fundamental rights that belong to the faithful in virtue of their status as human persons and of their insertion, ontological and sacramental, into the ecclesial community?

To discover the answer to this question, one must bear in mind that the matter of fundamental rights is, in every case but especially within the Church, bound up with the principle of dynamic growth, that unceasing progress of the Church which Paul VI, in his encyclical *Ecclesiam Suam,* called "reflection on itself" (i.e., the Church's progressive penetration of its own mystery); all the advances in man's knowledge of human nature, the evolution of the conditions of social life, etc., are other factors among those that exclude *a priori* any definitive and absolutely irreformable declaration of fundamental rights. On the other hand, if a fundamental law is to fulfill its proper juridico-positive function, it does demand, even when one is dealing with flexible constitutions, a high degree of stability and a certain measure of irreformability. From all this it follows that a declaration of fundamental rights in a constitutional canonical

---

[8] With regard to the right of association, there is a special significance to the replies of the commissions to the Council fathers' *modi;* in these answers it is described as *ius nativum* (in *Schema Decr. de apostolatu laicorum,* 1963) and as *iuri naturali consentaneum* (answer to modus 129, cap. II, *Decr. de Presbyterorum ministerio et vita,* 1965). Cf. A. del Portillo, "Ius associationis et associationes fidelium iuxta Concilii Vaticani II doctrinam," in *Ius Canonicum* 8 (1968), pp. 5-28.

text will necessarily bear the character of a *historic option* in virtue
of which the legislator, in the light of the basic principles of the
Church's sacramental nature and taking into account the signs
of the times, enumerates those rights of the faithful which can
be considered fundamental by reason of their universality and
their connection with a person's ontological-sacramental insertion into the People of God.

Given the limitations of the space available in this article, we
cannot discuss here the actual enumeration of these rights. All
we shall do therefore is to provide an example by quoting the
tentative general outline proposed by Viladrich. He classifies
these rights as follows:

1. a right to the spiritual riches of the Church and to all necessary aids to salvation, such as the sacraments, the Word of God,
etc.;

2. a right to take an active part in the life and purposes of the
Church;

3. a right to a spirituality of one's own;

4. a right to one's own rite;

5. a right to the exercise in their integrity of all personal
charisms;

6. a right to freely follow one's own ecclesial vocation (sacred,
lay or religious ministry);

7. a right to one's own apostolate;

8. a right of appeal to the hierarchy;

9. a right to express freely and publicly one's personal opinion on matters affecting the common good of the Church;

10. a right to information;

11. a right to Christian education, including its most specialized forms;

12. a right to legitimate freedom of research into the sacred
sciences and to the publication of one's conclusions;

13. a right to teach the sacred sciences;

14. a right of free association within the Church;

15. a right to legitimate autonomy within the temporal order.

III

The Protection of Rights

Obviously, a fundamental law that did no more than list the fundamental rights of the faithful would not be doing its job, not even in the restricted field that concerns us here. Enumerating and proclaiming fundamental rights can hardly be very effective unless accompanied by the setting up of a system of guarantees to protect them. From this point of view, what is needed is to analyze, with a thoroughness not possible in these pages, the total system of normative Canon Law, whose first principles ought to be written into the fundamental law itself. In the light of such an approach, it seems imperative:

1. to bring into full light the hierarchy of the various sources of Canon Law, in such a way as to establish a clear subordination of ordinary laws to the fundamental law. This subordination cannot be effective until such time as every legislator in the Church accepts, willingly or otherwise, certain formal criteria that make it easy to classify their normative acts, in such a way that it becomes possible to form a judgment on their constitutionality. A tradition of jurisprudence in the field of such judgments could be a liberating factor and counterbalance the danger of repressing initiative that is implicit in every text of positive law;

2. to establish a clear distinction between the functions of the various institutions within the Church,[9] thus rendering possible some kind of judicial revision of administrative acts;

3. to set up a system of appeal to ecclesiastical courts, guaranteeing to the faithful the protection of their rights from any abuse of authority that may arise and freeing those who govern the Church from the danger of pressure groups.

Only a juridical system that gives an effective guarantee of the fundamental rights of the faithful by making all, rulers and ruled,

[9] *Constitution on the Church in the Modern World,* n. 75.

subject to the law can adequately resolve the tensions manifest today in the life of the Church.

IV
THE SENSE OF THE CHURCH

The technical notions of State constitutional law and the doctrine of the Church on the way men should live together in the temporal order are of immeasurable value as material for a theory of fundamental rights within the Church and a most helpful precedent for future canonical legislation. One must nonetheless insist on the idea that, within the ecclesial community, the root of all fundamental rights is the ontological and sacramental state of the faithful. It is only on such a basis that any kind of canonical structure can be erected which takes into account the mystery of the Church, a methodological necessity recorded in a document of Vatican II.[10]

Given the impossibility in the present article of pursuing an ecclesiological analysis in sufficient detail, let it suffice to say that incorporation in the Church through baptism implies personal incorporation into Christ for each member of the faithful. That is why every truly fundamental entitlement either to powers or to rights has a sacramental basis within the Church. It follows that in this field one will always be treating of forms of entitlement that find their full sense in Christ. It remains true that their nature will necessarily be *vicarious* and their finality will be ordered to service to the community. These notions, traditional in the theology of pastoral powers, must also be taken into account when dealing with the implications of the common priesthood of all believers, and that is precisely the field within which the question of fundamental rights must be handled.

This aspect of the problem has to be born in mind when discussing how to apply to the ecclesial community the theory of fundamental rights, because any failure to do justice to the spe-

[10] *Decree on Priestly Training,* n. 16.

cialized form in which the question is posed from within the life of the Church could lead to a distorted perspective. It must not be forgotten that the whole idea of fundamental rights has taken shape in the field of secular jurisprudence as the result of claims arising in the context of the tension between State and individual. This way of posing the question has to be transcended in Canon Law, because any understanding of such rights that implied a dialectical attitude toward the solidarity of the community or a state of tension would be doing violence to the unity of the body of Christ *quod est Ecclesia* (Col. 1. 18).

Therefore, the proclamation of fundamental rights within the Church cannot be taken as the concession, in due form of law, of the faithful's demand for spheres of autonomy, an autonomy to be exercised by them in dialectical tension with pastoral authority. Rather, it must be understood as the outcome of an historic option on the part of the legislator, an option made in the context of the present particular stage of the Church's pilgrimage through time. The purpose of this option is to recast into the most technically adequate form the community's juridical order, whose task is to safeguard, in a way compatible with diversity of ministries, *aequalitas quoad dignitatem et actionem cunctis fidelibus communem circa aedificationem Corporis Christi* ("equality in dignity and in that activity common to all the faithful in the building up of the body of Christ").[11]

[11] *Constitution on the Church*, n. 32.

Bruno Primetshofer, C.SS.R. / *Linz, Austria*

The Right of Assembly in Canon Law

I

GENERAL CONSIDERATIONS

Along with the right of association, the right of assembly (freedom of assembly) is one of the basic rights in a democratic legal system. In the history of human thought and constitutional government, these rights are included among the "classical" civil rights, having their purely extrinsic basis in constitutional law. They are embodied in Article 20 of the 1948 U.N. Declaration, and in Article 11 of the European Declaration on the Rights of Man (1950).

By the right of assembly we mean the capacity of citizens to band together for the attainment of certain goals, without having to obtain prior authorization from somewhere else. The right of assembly is logically tied up with freedom of speech and the right of petition; if there were no constitutional guarantee of the latter rights, the right of assembly would be fairly meaningless. This logical tieup finds clear expression in the first constitutional document that is relevant here. In the First Amendment to the U.S. Constitution (1791), freedom of assembly is immediately associated with freedom of speech and the right of petition.[1]

As is often the case with basic rights, their concrete exercise

[1] W. Mallmann, *Vereins- und Versammlungsfreiheit* VIII (Freiburg im Br., ⁶1963), pp. 106ff.

tends to depend less on the codified legal formulation than on the interpretation of the legislator and their fate in judiciary practice. The basic right of free assembly can also be found in the Constitutions of the Soviet Socialist Republic and China, but this does not tell us anything about the actual exercise of this right. However much the codified formulations may echo one another in talking about freedom of association and freedom of assembly, the concrete results depend on the role accorded to these rights in the concrete practice of daily living. In democratic systems, the rights of association and assembly flow from the rights of the human person and belong to the individual. In "Peoples' Democracies", by contrast, these rights are viewed as "socialistic human rights" designed to serve the all-pervasive communist system.[2]

II
THE RIGHT OF ASSEMBLY IN CODIFIED CANON LAW

Is the basic right of assembly grounded in Canon Law, and if so, to what extent? These are not easy questions to answer. At the very outset we must give up the notion that it is expressly guaranteed as a *basic right* in the same way that it is formulated in civil constitutions. The reason is that the distinction between constitutional and common law, evident in civil government is alien to the Code of Canon Law insofar as the two types of law are not set off from one another in any external way.

Although canonical theory has maintained the distinction for some time and to some extent, it is interesting to note that the phrase "constitutional law" crops up for the first time in universal Church law only after Vatican II. We find it first in Paul VI's Apostolic Letter *De episcoporum muneribus,* where the bishop's powers of dispensation are discussed.[3] The paradox is that this new distinction introduces a conceptual model of a legal order

[2] *Ibid.*
[3] Paul VI, Apostolic Letter *De episcoporum muneribus* (June 15, 1966); *Osterreichisches Archiv für Kirchenrecht* 17 (1966), p. 367.

whose basic features and presuppositions have not yet been worked up. Thus it is difficult to say in a given case what is to be regarded as constitutional law and what is not.

In Canon Law we do not even find freedom of assembly expressly formulated as a *basic legal principle*. Our only recourse is to plod through the existing norms to see whether something may be deduced from them concerning the right of assembly.

According to a fairly sizable number of commentators, the right of assembly finds implicit expression in Canon 684. Since this canon says that the faithful are doing something praiseworthy when they participate in associations that are established or at least approved by the Church, we can conclude that there can be associations of the faithful formed of their own free will rather than by the hierarchy. That the Code of Canon Law does prescribe the right of assembly is seen more clearly in canonical developments and clarifications since the Code than in Canon 684.

On November 4, 1918, about six months after the Code came into force, the Consistorial Congregation prescribed a new format for the quinquennial diocesan reports. Here a careful distinction was made between associations of the faithful established by ecclesiastical authority (and hence subject to the jurisdiction of the local Ordinary), and other associations (*associationes sociales*) that were only under the general direction of the local ordinary.[4]

What was the extent of this overall guidance to be? Clarification came several years later when a dispute arose over the St. Vincent de Paul Society that had been founded by Antoine Frederic Ozanam. In reaching a decision on the proper degree of episcopal control over such an association, the Congregation of the Council noted several things. Among them was the fact that besides the associations established and approved by Church authorities, there were also associations that were under the exclusive control and direction of the laity; such associations were merely recommended or praised by the Church. Thus such

[4] *Acta Apostolicae Sedis* X (1918), p. 502.

associations were not officially recognized by the Church, and they were not under the direction of Church authorities; they were under the control of the laity and governed by their own by-laws.[5]

In the view of most commentators, the laity's right of assembly, which is implicitly contained in Canon 684, has found clear expression in subsequent legal clarifications pertaining to the Code of Canon Law. In the light of the aforementioned decision of the Congregation of the Council, canonical theory distinguishes between public and private associations; the former are those established by Church authorities, the latter are those established by private groups or individuals.[6]

Before we go on to consider the new canonical developments during and after Vatican II, let us take a brief look at the general background surrounding the codification of Canon Law. It is somewhat surprising that the ecclesaistical legislator neglected to mention the right of assembly in the codification of Canon Law. This is particularly true because, long before the Code of Canon Law was promulgated, there had been explicit references to man's right to associate freely and form groups on his own—this right flowing from human nature itself.

As early as Pope Leo XIII's Encyclical *Libertas praestantissimum,* we read that man, by his very nature, joins with others to accomplish things he cannot manage by himself. In the Encyclical *Rerum novarum,* the right of assembly as such is expressly called for. But the addressee of these demands was the civil State and its law code, and it is worth pointing out that these postulates were raised at a time when many nations in Europe and elsewhere had already incorporated the right of assembly in their constitutions. Now when the codification of Canon Law was taking place in the early 20th century, a host of civil codes from the 18th and 19th centuries were available as models for the

[5] *S. Congregatio Concilii,* diocese of Corrientes (November 13, 1920); *Acta Apostolicae Sedis* XIII (1921), pp. 135 and 44.

[6] G. Onclin, "Principia generalia de fidelium associationibus," in *Apollinaris* 36 (1963), p. 85.

ecclesiastical legislator.[7] Yet, surprisingly enough, the basic
notion of freedom of assembly was not expressly formulated in
the Code.

This paradoxical situation has been the subject of much com-
ment, and various explanations are offered. The explanation of
Nell-Breuning seems to be as sound as any. He points out that
the doctrine of democracy and popular sovereignty, the ultimate
foundation for the right of assembly, found its way only very
slowly into the Church's official doctrine of the State. For a long
time the Church was inclined to identify the structure of the
State as closely as possible with her own divinely ordained structure, in order to show the close relationship and inter-connec-
tion between the social structure of both.[8] And as long as one
sees the power of the State as something analogous to the hierarchical composition of the Church—i.e., as something operating from the top down—the proper ground has not been prepared
for incorporating the right of assembly into the legal system. For
the latter step stems from the presupposition that union results
solely from the consent of the "governed", that it can take shape
with a minimum of juridical formality and without the consent
and approval of a hierarchically higher placed sovereign.

The Church sees herself as a hierarchically ordered community, in which rights devolve not from the people but from a
commissioned authority. This authority is not delegated by the
people; he is ultimately the representative of God himself. This
view may have been the reason why no explicit mention was
made of the right of assembly. Deep down, the legislator may
have sensed the logical connection between the right of assembly
and the right of petition, and this may also have been a factor.

The Church's conception of herself, however, does leave
room for incorporating the right of assembly into law. To con-

[7] F. Elsener, "Der Codex Iuris Canonici im Rahmen der europäischen
Kodifikationsgeschichte," in A. Müller, F. Elsener and P. Huizing, *Vom
Kirchenrecht zur Kirchenordnung?* (Einsiedeln-Zürich-Cologne, 1968),
p. 38.

[8] O. von Nell-Breuning, *Lexicon für Theologie und Kirche* III (Freiburg im Br., ²1968), p. 524.

clude that the hierarchical structure of the Church rules out the right of assembly is to misread the facts and draw the wrong conclusion.

III
THE RIGHT OF ASSEMBLY AND VATICAN II

As we have already noted, the right of assembly was not expressly established in the Code of Canon Law. Instead, it may be deduced from Canon 684 and subsequent clarifications of the Code. In the teachings of Vatican II, by contrast, the right of assembly is expressly mentioned in several places. Two general types of statements can be discerned: (1) those in which the Council, referring explicitly to earlier papal statements, proclaims that the right of assembly is a basic right of the human person in civil society; [9] (2) those in which the right of assembly is set forth mainly with the latter statements, insofar as they deal with the laity and the clergy.

The Laity

The most important statement is to be found in the *Decree on the Apostolate of the Laity* (n. 19). Noting the proliferation of institutions and the rapid pace of modern society, the Council points out the need for new apostolic initiatives from Catholics that would be international in scope. It then stipulates that "lay people have a right to form organizations, manage them, and join them, provided they maintain the proper relationship to ecclesiastical authority".

This passage is interesting from a canonical standpoint because of the accompanying footnote (n. 31 in the Decree). It refers to the decision of the Sacred Congregation of the Council mentioned earlier in this article, but it does not allude to Canon

[9] *Constitution on the Church in the Modern World,* nn. 68 and 75. See also A. Del Portillo, "Ius associationis et associationes fidelium iuxta Concilii Vaticani II doctrinam," in *Ius Canonicum* VIII (1968), pp. 8ff.

684 of the Code. It thus suggests that the right of assembly is
expressed more clearly in the Congregational decision than in
Canon 684.

This conciliar passage represents the first expressed statement
about the laity's right of assembly. Perhaps even more significant
is the fact that it clearly represents a new approach in setting
forth the rights of the laity, as opposed to the approach in the
Code. The Code has often been criticized for the fact that its
norms seem to be almost exclusively concerned with the rights
and privileges of the clergy. For example, the only canon that
talks about a *right* of the laity in the relevant section is Canon
682, which discusses their right to demand proper spiritual remedies and the means of salvation from the clergy according to the
norms of ecclesiastical discipline. The formulation of this canon
was justly criticized at the First Synod of Bishops (Rome, Autumn
1967), where critics pointed out that, in defining the rights of the
laity, it is not enough to subsume them under the corresponding
obligation of the clergy.[10]

In the conciliar decree, by contrast, the right of assembly is
expressly set forth as a right of the laity, independent of the consent of the clergy and not originating therein. It is presented as
a *ius nativum*, having its foundation in human nature itself. This
fact may be seen more clearly from the whole complex of conciliar statements and from the background history of this particular passage than from its final wording. As early as the preliminary schema of 1962, the right of assembly was viewed as a
right rooted in, and deriving from, the social nature of man.[11]

The intent of the Council fathers to present the right of assembly
as a *ius nativum* becomes even clearer when we look at the sug-
gested changes (*modi*) that were not adopted. Some wanted to
introduce such qualifying statements as "with the approval of
Church authorities", "with the prior authorization of Church

---

[10] R. Laurentin, *Le premier Synode: Histoire et bilan* (Paris, 1968),
p. 81.

[11] Portillo, *op. cit.*, p. 10.

authorities", and "without prejudice to the rights of Church authorities". These *modi* were disregarded; the final version presents the right of assembly as something belonging to the laity without the prior authorization of ecclesiastical authorities.[12]

At this point one is sorely tempted to delve into the juridical consequences of the right of assembly for any new revision of Canon Law. To stay within the proper bounds of this article, however, I shall not go into such details here.[13]

The Clergy

There is another question to be considered here. Does this explicit right of assembly belong only to the laity, or is it a right of the clergy as well? In other words, do the principles of Vatican II apply to only one segment of the People of God? In the pertinent literature, interestingly enough, the right of assembly is viewed as a specifically lay right. The question of the clergy's right in this regard is all the more justified because a papal pronouncement, denying the right of assembly to clerics, was issued scarcely a decade before the promulgation of the Code of Canon Law.

In his Encyclical *Pascendi,* Pius X ordered that bishops should very rarely (*rarissime*) permit the free association of clerics—in view of the rising tide of modernism. When such permission was given, the gatherings were not to deal with any subjects that were the province of the bishop or the Apostolic See. Along with this prohibition, a *consilium de vigilantia* was established to scrutinize the writings of Catholic authors. Such authors were not to make any statements that hinted at new ecclesiastical regulations or that called for a new Christian humanism and a new social vocation for the clergy.[14] On March 22, 1918, the Holy Office further approved measures relating to the

---

[12] *Ibid.,* pp. 11f.

[13] Again we refer the reader to the instructive study of Portillo (*op. cit.,* pp. 12ff.), where he discusses this question in a section entitled *Consequentiae de iure condendo.*

[14] *Archiv für katholisches Kirchenrecht* 88 (1908), p. 142.

watchdog committee, even though they had not been mentioned
in the Code of Canon Law.[15]

Considering all this, one might well have asked himself
whether the papal prohibition on clerical assembly, which is
logically tied up with the watchdog recommendation, still held
true in the codification of Canon Law. We find a "no" answer to
this question in the norms of the Code of Canon Law,[16] and it
has been definitively laid to rest by Vatican II. The Council
accords the right of assembly to the clergy, and it even goes so
far as to recommend such associations.[17]

The juridical status of these associations was the subject of
much debate, especially with regard to the proper degree of
episcopal control over them. The majority of bishops wanted to
set some sort of limitation on the clergy's right of assembly, per-
mitting only those associations that were established by the
bishop or subordinate to an episcopal conference. This objection
was dismissed by the commission in charge of the schema, for
it pointed out that clerics could not be deprived of a right that
was presented as a natural one for the laity.[18]

The clergy's right of assembly, however, does not have the
same scope as that of the laity. While the *Decree on the Apostolate of the Laity* talks about maintaining "the proper relationship
to ecclesiastical authority", the *Decree on the Ministry and Life
of Priests* talks about "officially approved" associations of clerics.[19]
There is some juridical vagueness in both expressions, to be sure,
but it is clear that the clergy do not enjoy the same degree of
freedom in this matter as do the laity.

The basis for this difference lies in the special obligation of
obedience that secular and order priests undertake toward the

[15] *Ibid.*, pp. 143f.
[16] K. Mörsdorf, *Lehrbuch des Kirchenrechts auf Grund des Codex
Iuris Canonici* I (Munich-Paderborn-Vienna, [11]1964), p. 564; Portillo,
op. cit., p. 26.
[17] *Decree on the Ministry and Life of Priests*, n. 7.
[18] See the schema of the conciliar *Decree on the Ministry and Life of
Priests* cited by Portillo, *op. cit.*, p. 26.
[19] *Decree on the Ministry and Life of Priests*, n. 8.

THE RIGHT OF ASSEMBLY IN CANON LAW 99

bishop of the diocese. This obligation arises from the fact of ordination itself, and it does not matter here whether a special relationship of *canonical* service enters the picture or not. The *Decree on the Ministry and Life of Priests* alludes to this obligation of service when it notes that "the priests of the New Testament, through the sacrament of orders, have the sublime and much needed office of fathers and teachers among God's people" (n. 9). While many individual charisms and types of services are clearly necessary, "priests serving the same diocese form a single presbytery under their own bishop" (n. 8).[20] Herein lies the basis for limiting the clergy's right of assembly to some degree, but it certainly does not involve any scrupulous watchdog action.

What is the significance of the right that has now been expressly accorded to the laity and the clergy? What does the right of assembly bode for the future? To begin with, many hope that in the near future all these scattered rights based on man's freedom and dignity will be compiled into an ecclesiastical code of basic constitutional rights.[21] Insofar as the right of assembly itself is concerned, it seems to be of particular importance in the present-day pastoral situation. History has repeatedly shown that freely undertaken pastoral initiatives, leaping beyond parochial and diocesan boundaries, have often had more impact than initiatives organized along strict lines.

Consider the awesome pastoral situation in huge metropolitan areas, which can no longer be handled with the old concept of the parish. Here freely organized groups, designed to create and handle specific areas of pastoral activity, could take on increased importance. The plurality of our present-day society, as well as the concomitant shift from neighborhood church to freely-chosen church, calls for the creation of a pastoral effort that will be

[20] See P. J. Cordes, *Lexicon für Theologie und Kirche* III, *op. cit.*, p. 180.

[21] See J. Neumann, "Uber die Notwendigkeit eines gesamtkirchlichen Grundgesetzes," in *Theologie im Wandel* (1967), pp. 423ff.; *idem*, "Revision der Kirchenverfassung," in *Wort und Wahrheit* 23 (1968), pp. 390ff.

highly effective with all the varied categories of people around. Canon Law can contribute to this effort by putting the stress where it properly belongs. Hopefully, an earnest nurturing of the right of assembly will proceed hand in hand with dynamic pastoral efforts, adapted to the needs of the day.

Jan Rietmeijer, S.J./*Nijmegen, Netherlands*

The Competence of the Bishop in Matters of Dispensation

The following thoughts were prompted by the question whether, in a case where a papal dispensation could reasonably be expected for a priest but the application in Rome entailed grave difficulties, the bishop himself could give this dispensation. That this problem arises frequently in the present situation of celibacy seems obvious. On the one hand, those in touch with priests who in conscience think they have to get married will understand the very serious arguments moving such priests to this conclusion which is often the only human—and therefore Christian—solution for them. On the other hand, there is the long wait for a dispensation from Rome, which often takes a great deal of time and implies such grave difficulties as loss of a job, a painful situation for the family, the loss of reputation and serious damage because of the psychological tensions to which the priest has already been exposed and which the long wait makes gradually intolerable.

In such a situation the question naturally arises whether the bishop should not have the competence and the function to act according to the needs created by the situation. It is equally clear that this question reaches beyond the concrete situation and affects the whole problem of dispensation in Canon Law. The history of the Church shows that this problem has arisen whenever the situation changed in both the Church and the world.

Now that Vatican II has so clearly shown that the Church is confronted with a new age, it is necessary to rethink this old problem in the light of the values stressed and rediscovered at that Council.

Church Order before Vatican II

The general principle for dispensation in Church law has been laid down in Canon 80 of the present Code. Dispensation can only be granted by the legislator or his successor or a higher authority. In strict logic this means that, since the pope is considered the legislator with regard to the general laws of the Church, the ordinaries under the pope (for practical purposes, the bishops) have no competence whatever here unless it has been given them implicitly or explicitly. This conclusion is confirmed by Canon 81 which adds that the regulation cannot be disregarded "even in an exceptional case". It is true that there are several examples in the Code where such competence is explicitly granted (in connection with marriage, for instance— see Canons 1028 and 1043-45), but the most general and striking case is that mentioned in section 2 of Canon 81 for exceptional cases: when it is difficult to get in touch with the Holy See, when delay is dangerous and when the matter concerns a dispensation usually granted by the Holy See, the bishop himself can grant it. This seems to answer the question stated at the beginning insofar as Church law is concerned before Vatican II. For it is a known fact that Rome has practically never dispensed a priest from celibacy. It is an open question whether it has happened in secret (*forum internum*), but this is irrelevant here because such an eventuality is presumed to be strictly secret.

Since the obligation to celibacy is linked with the ordination to the subdiaconate, the question can be asked whether, at least in the case of deacons and subdeacons, the bishop could dispense, given the circumstances mentioned in Canon 81, section 2. Since in these cases the dispensation was easily granted by Rome, one would expect that the answer would be in the affirmative. But in 1949 the Commission of Cardinals, charged with the authentic interpretation of the Code, replied to a submitted question that the bishop's competence and the circumstances referred to in section 2 of Canon 81 did not cover the granting of dispensations in matters of reserved vows and the obligation to celibacy imposed on deacons and subdeacons.[1]

This at first sight curiously restrictive interpretation leads one to look for the motivation behind it. According to the relevant literature on this subject, the reason was twofold, a practical one and a more speculative one. During the war the bishops had quietly granted dispensation from celibacy in the case of deacons and subdeacons, basing themselves on this section 2 of Canon 81. Immediately after the war the centralizing tendency in matters of Church law reached its climax, and in this light one can understand this strict interpretation. A confirmation of this view is found in the curious interpretation by the same commission, equally inspired by what happened during the war—namely that the condition "if it is difficult to get in touch with Rome" does not apply if it can still be done via the nuncio.[2] The more speculative reason may have been the opinion, widespread before Vatican II, that dispensation from celibacy was not only a dispensation from a positive ecclesiastical law but also a dispensation from some implicit vow linked with the ordination to the subdiaconate. Together with the teaching about the pope's *vicaria potestas* (vicarious power) it may have led to this strict reservation, even in the case of subdeacons and deacons.

The Church order before Vatican II shows that the principle that only the legislator can dispense from his own laws was carried through with uncompromising logic. This principle, already formulated before Gratian, was defended in this medieval author's writings [3] and maintained because of the great prestige of his *Decretum* throughout the following centuries, though not always with the same consistency. The powers allotted to the bishops in the Code and reaffirmed in their "faculties" took the

[1] Comm. Cod., Jan. 26, 1949: *AAS* 41 (1949), p. 158.
[2] Comm. Cod., June 26, 1947: *AAS* 39 (1947), p. 374.
[3] Dict. post c. 16, C. XXV, qu. 1.

edge off this harsh system. For the powers granted in the Code were considered to belong to the *potestas ordinaria* (ordinary power) of the bishop, but this is still different from recognizing powers as inherent in the office before the existence of any Code. It is precisely on this point that Vatican II shed a new light.

Church Order after Vatican II

The documents of Vatican II clearly show that this principle of the Code has been replaced by another. Not only the legislator can dispense (while others can do so only by implicit or explicit authorization), but the bishops can always dispense from general ecclesiastical laws unless the highest authority reserves such a dispensation especially to itself. The *Decree on the Pastoral Office of Bishops in the Church* states: "Except when it is a question of matters reserved to the supreme authority of the Church, the general law of the Church gives each diocesan bishop the faculty to grant dispensations in particular cases to the faithful over whom he exercises authority according to the norm of the law, provided he judges it helpful for their spiritual welfare" (n. 8). This clearly "derogates from Canon 81", at least the first section of it, as is stated in the Motu Proprio of June 15, 1966, entitled *De episcoporum muneribus* ("On the Functions of the Bishops"), which was meant to put the conciliar decree into practice.[4] This Motu Proprio is interesting not only because of the list of cases reserved to Rome but also because of the introductory statements, which I shall come back to later.

However, for our question about whether a bishop can dispense a priest from celibacy, it is important to know that the Motu Proprio reserves this power to the Holy See. The list of reserved cases mentions "the obligation to celibacy or the prohibition of marriage which binds deacons and priests, even when they have lawfully been reduced to or have returned to the

[4] Motu Proprio, *De episcoporum muneribus*, June 15, 1966: *AAS* 57, pp. 467-72.

lay state" (IX, 1). Then it also mentions "the impediment to marriage arising from ordination to the diaconate or the priesthood, or from the solemn religious profession" (IX, 2). In contrast with the previous practice, Rome now regularly grants dispensation from celibacy to priests, on condition that they promise to cease exercising their ministry.

On February 2, 1964, the Congregation of Doctrine, then still called the Holy Office, sent out an instruction about the procedure to be followed by an episcopal curia to institute the process necessary for a dispensation from celibacy. The attached questionnaires were still wholly dominated by the mentality of the previous processes concerning an ordination "under duress" (Canon 214). In that case it was possible, after proven evidence of the facts, to obtain a declaration from the Holy See that in this situation the burdens of ordination to the priesthood had not been accepted. During more recent years, however, it has become clear that dispensation is both justified and desirable on grounds of equity—that is, when in practice it is necessary (e.g., when a marriage has been decided upon). Therefore, now that Rome frequently dispenses from celibacy, the question comes up again about Canon 81, section 2: Do we not have here the special circumstances where the bishop himself can dispense?

It is clear that the conciliar Decree has not abolished this section of Canon 81, and this is confirmed by the fact that it is spelled out in the Motu Proprio already mentioned: "The statement of the conciliar Decree *Christus Dominus* only partially modifes Canon 81" (II). I have just mentioned this modification and what it contains. It seems therefore that in a particular case all the conditions of Canon 81, section 2, may be fulfilled for an episcopal dispensation, apart from one objection: the reply given by the Commission on the Interpretation of the Code of 1949. From the strictly legal point of view there might be a doubt, because this statement was not explicitly revoked, which seems necessary if I read the words of the Motu Proprio rightly: "Those laws laid down by the Church in the Code of Canon Law, and not subsequently revoked, we declare still in force in their totality unless the Second Vatican Council has explicitly abolished them or wholly or partially modified them" (II).

Yet there are very serious grounds for considering that this decision of the Commission of the Interpretation of the Code has lost its force. First of all, that reply spoke of dispensation of deacons and subdeacons, while in the present document the subdeacons are not mentioned at all and priests are explicitly included. Moreover, and this is more important, the basis of this reply has collapsed. It is quite clear from the conciliar documents that the Fathers rejected the theory about the implicit vow contained in the ordination to the subdiaconate. As proof we may mention that in the above-mentioned reserved cases there is not a single reference to the argument about the vow, unless one wants to imply it in the general introductory statement: "The term 'ecclesiastical law' in no way covers those matters of positive or natural divine law where only the pope can dispense, if he has the vicarious power, as happens in the dispensation from a contracted but not consummated marriage, or in the matter of the Pauline privilege, and other matters" (V).

That these "other matters" would include the celibacy of the priesthood cannot be presupposed but would have to be proved. The invalidating impediment to marriage constituted by celibacy is obviously a purely positive law, and the implied obligation not to marry must without doubt also be considered as a purely positive law according to the conciliar and post-conciliar documents. There is not a word about an obligation based on a vow in the *Decree on the Ministry and Life of Priests,* which simply says: "In the Latin Church it was imposed by law on all who were to be promoted to sacred orders" (n. 16). The same holds for the *Decree on Priestly Training* where there is at most an allusion to a charismatic gift, linked with the law: "May they deeply sense how gratefully this state deserves to be undertaken, not only as a requisite of Church law but as a precious gift which should be humbly sought from God" (n. 10). Nor is there any reference to such a vow in the encyclical on celibacy of June 24,

1967.[5] All this shows that basis of the argument used in the decision of 1949 by the Commission on the Code has collapsed, and with it the force of the decision itself.

When we look at the Church order after the Council as a whole, we see that at Vatican II a new principle emerged with regard to dispensation from ecclesiastical laws, that the consequences of this principle are often not accepted, and that the operation of this principle is frequently hampered by the persistence of pre-conciliar canonical structures. I would therefore like to suggest another approach.

Toward a New Church Order

Today we have become aware of the fact that it is possible to make changes in structures which until recently were considered to be fixed for all time. And so there is a tendency to look at the more distant past to see whether these structures were in fact as immutable as was taken for granted. Vatican II reassessed the episcopal office and drew conclusions about the bishop's competence in matters of dispensation which clearly contradict the Code of 1918. It is therefore interesting to see that in the past, too, this function has been seen in a different light.

It is impossible to give even a summary survey of this question in the history of Canon Law. It has received masterly treatment up to the 14th century at the hands of Stiegler [6] and Brys.[7] I only want to mention briefly the following points. If, during the first centuries, the bishops obviously granted dispensations when necessary, and continued to do so later, and even if Rome, too, was approached for dispensations, it is clear that the decisive factor here was the bishop's care for the community entrusted to him. Even when later, particularly in the 10th and 11th

[5] Encyclical *Sacerdotalis coelibatus*, June 24, 1967: *AAS* 58 (1967), pp. 219f.

[6] M. A. Stiegler, *Dispensation, Dispensationswesen und Dispensationsrecht im Kirchenrecht geschichtlich dargestellt* (Mainz, 1901).

[7] J. Brys, *De dispensatione in jure canonico praesertim apud decretistas et decretalistas usque ad medium saeculum decimum quartum* (Bruges, 1925).

centuries, the popes insisted that they were the rightful granters of
dispensations because discipline had become very slack, we still
see how freely and openly contemporary authors wrote about the
competence and functions of the bishops.

Here Ivo of Chartres had a decisive influence. In the Prologue
to his Decree, known as the *Decretum Ivonis*,[8] he was the first to
deal systematically with dispensation in Church laws, and he
frequently referred to this statement in his letters.[9] He states
that the law is not an end in itself and that love is always above
the law. For this reason dispensation is "laudable and especially
salutary".[10] The granting of dispensations is a duty of ecclesiastical authority, "because where salvation is at stake, one must
not only look for the remedy to the harsh law but also apply the
instrument of dispensation to calm the storms, and this is a means
which is never despised by human beings".[11] For Ivo, the sole
criterion remains love: "Because love is the fulfillment of the law,
we believe that the laws are obeyed there where we recognize that
the mandate of love has been fulfilled."[12] In similar terms he
says in his Prologue: "When, in considering laws and dispensations, love, the fullness of the law, is taken as the criterion, we
shall neither err nor sin, and when in one way or another we
deviate from the strict course of law (*rigor juris*), love will acquit
us."[13] From these texts and all his letters it is clear that Ivo
regards as the characteristic function of the bishop the measure-
ment of the strictness of the law against the mercy of dispensation
(*misericordia dispensationis*). And he repeats it once again in no

[8] *Prologus et Decretum Ivonis: PL* 161.
[9] *Litterae Ivonis: PL* 162.
[10] Ep. 236, *loc. cit.*, p. 242: "Laudabilis et saluberrima dispensatio."
[11] "Non enim in tanto salutis periculo solus medicinae rigor servandus
est, sed et dispensationis modus, qui nulli sapienti displicuit, ad sedandas
tantas perturbationes in aliquibus admittendus est" (Ep. 214, p. 218).
[12] "Cum enim plenitudo legis sit caritas, in hoc legibus obtemperatum
esse credimus, in quo caritatis opus impletum esse cognovimus" (Ep. 190,
p. 196).
[13] "Si quis quod legerit de sanctionibus sive de dispensationibus eccles-
iasticis, ad caritatem, quae est plenitudo legis, referat, non errabit, non
peccabit, et quando aliqua ratione a summo rigore declinabit, caritas ex-
cusabit" (*Decr. Ivonis: PL* 161, p. 58).

uncertain terms: "Since the rulers [i.e., bishops] are entrusted with maintaining the rigor of the law according to the requirements of time and place . . . they can also grant dispensations out of regard for the person or for the good of the community as long as there is no offense given to the Church of God. In all this the rulers should take every care that they do not allow what can be harmful and prevent what can be fruitful." [14]

Ivo's liberal language, when he speaks of the function of the "princes of the Church" (which, for him, was linked with applying to Rome for dispensations), was overshadowed by the enforcement of centralization by the medieval popes in the centuries that followed. But even then that personal responsibility of the local bishop appears time and again. Practically all the Decretalists teach that the power to grant dispensations belongs exclusively to the pope, always on the ground that this power flows from the supreme legislative authority,[15] and yet, they recognize that the bishops, too, have a certain power to dispense, although only in a small degree, "where they do not have the plenitude of power but are only called to a partial function".[16] With these Decretalists the sounds of the past are heard again, though in a very different context. From the fact that the bishop could grant dispensation from the penal laws, they concluded— mistakenly—that the bishops could grant dispensations in general if they had not been explicitly forbidden to do so. This teaching was soon rejected, but since the Decretalist method always included "existing opinion", it was constantly quoted and passed on, so that we find it frequently in the great Decretalists of later times, such as Sanchez and de Soto and so many others.

It seems reasonable to see in this an indication that sheer cen-

---

[14] "Verum quia sicut rigor commissus est rectoribus ad servandum pro necessitate locorum et temporum . . . sic dispensationes eisdem permissae sunt, quae Ecclesiae Dei non generent scandalum pro honestate personarum, aut pro utilitate rerum publicarum. In quibus omnibus adhibenda est rectorum diligentia, ut nec nocitura concedant, nec profutura prohibeant" (Ep. 231, p. 235).

[15] Cf. Brys, op cit., pp. 138-40.

[16] "Cum illi non habeant 'plenitudinem potestatis' sed tantum 'in partem' sollicitudinis sint vocati": Brys, op. cit., p. 143.

tralization was never found wholly satisfactory and that, in one way or another, it was always felt that dispensation was part of the bishop's function. Even after Trent and in the later canonists this deeper view remained alive. Thus, for instance, Barbosa recognized that "customary law can make a dispensation valid which would not be so in other circumstances".[17] And although this canonical lawyer does not agree with this opinion, he reproduces in detail the opinion of others, according to which bishops can do by divine right in their own diocese all that the pope can do in the whole Church, unless the pope has made an explicit reservation.[18]

And so we see how this theory, though based on a mistaken interpretation as already mentioned, had a vast influence. It is obvious that Gallicans and Febronians would seize on it to vindicate the power of the bishop against the so-called centuries-old usurpation of power by Rome. If in the end this theory was condemned in its consequences in connection with the errors of the Synod of Pistoia,[19] this does not explain away the fact that the motive which lay behind it—namely, that the bishop needs the power of dispensation to govern his diocese—was extremely important. In other words, whether the arguments used were right or wrong, all these authors came back to the basis for the bishop's competence to grant dispensation, and this competence rests on his *pastoral function,* in order that, as Reiffenstuel argued so convincingly, "the sheep entrusted to the pastor should not be deprived of the necessary help in their needs".[20]

The teaching of Vatican II about the pastoral office and the "personal competence" of the bishop is therefore in line with the best teaching of the past, even though it was rather forgotten. The Council brought this truth out again, as the Motu Proprio fully recognized: "The pastoral function—that is, the constant and daily solicitude for the flock—is transmitted to the bishops as

[17] Barbosa, *De officio et potestate Episcopi. Compendium,* n. 75 (Lyons, 1724), p. 171a.

[18] Barbosa, *op. cit.,* p. 379a.

[19] Cf. *Denz.* 2606 and 2607.

[20] Cf. Reiffenstuel, Lib. I, tit. 2, n. 470 (Rome, 1831), p. 134b.

envoys of Christ himself with a personal, ordinary and direct
competence, for the sake of which they have the sacred right and
the duty before God to legislate, pronounce judgment and regulate all that belongs to worship and the apostolate for their subjects." [21]

Theology and Church Order

Vatican II's new formulation of the bishop's competence to
dispense in matters of general law reveals a very different
approach from that of the 1918 Code. But if we look at it from
the purely canonical angle, it may seem that we have here merely
a reversion of the burden of proof: in the Code the bishop cannot do anything unless it has been granted him, while in Vatican
II he can do everything unless it has been withdrawn from him.
A closer look at the whole body of conciliar texts shows, however,
that these texts are inspired by another theology. The careful
reassessment of the specific function of the bishop simply had
to lead to another view of dispensation in matters of general law.
Lederer [22] is therefore right when he says: "The question of the
bishop's power to grant dispensation from a general law of the
Church in a particular situation cannot be decided by juridical
principles alone. It depends essentially on the God-given mission
of the bishops within the Church. It is therefore just as much a
theological question as a juridical one, a view which broke
through time and again during the Council." [23]

The most striking feature of this new theology in this connection is that the view of positive Canon Law as the ultimate
criterion has become wholly unacceptable and that every
canonical structure, however important, must remain subordinate
to the principles which precede such a structure. Before everything we have the service of the Gospel, or, in other words, the
sacramental bond of all with Christ the Lord. Christians are not
one insofar as they constitute an association but insofar as they

---

[21] Motu Proprio *De episcoporum muneribus: AAS* 57 (1966), p. 467.
[22] J. Lederer, "Die Neuordnung des Dispensrechtes," in *AfkKR* 135 (1966), pp. 415-43.
[23] *Ibid.,* p. 417.

are one with the Lord of the Church. Thus pope and bishops do not constitute a governing college because they try, in one way or another, to cooperate as closely as possible, but because together they are one with the Lord in the way he willed it. Every Christian community, gathered around the Word and the table of the Lord, above all owes obedience to the faith and has as its first and last criterion the love of Christ.

Thus pope and bishops do not simply operate by the rules of a given legal system which they hope that ultimately the Lord will make evangelically fruitful through love. No, in all decisions evangelical love stands as the criterion above all human agreements and systems. In this sense the antinomy between the legal Church and the loving Church is abolished in the Church of the Lord, and abolished in principle, and not as if some *deus ex machina* will ensure that all legal structures will ultimately serve the cause of love. Thus the legal Church—inevitable as a human society—remains always subordinate to the summons and the ultimately and actually decisive judgment of the Lord's love in the concrete situation.

In regard to our subject matter, this means first of all that the bishop has a personal power, a personal responsibility to the Lord which cannot be taken away from him and of which neither the Church nor the pope will ever deprive him. Is this direct functional obedience to the Lord not really the concrete expression (and therefore more intelligible in our days) of the traditional teaching about the "divine right" of the episcopal office? Therefore, as Lederer again rightly observes,[24] the expression that every bishop is "given" the "power" to grant dispensations is unfortunate and derives from the structure of a Church order that belongs to the past. A more concrete arrangement must be found to ensure that the unity of the pope as the supreme pastor with the local pastors can function as well as possible. "The same theological factor may be perfectly clear in itself, but can be expressed in various concrete ways, while it is not always

[24] *Ibid.*, p. 419.

evident which way is the best." [25] Yet one thing remains certain: any arrangement will remain subordinate to the judgment of obedience in faith and the judgment of love. Who does not see here the constantly repeated insistence of Ivo that love is the fulfillment of the law (*plenitudo legis*)? Even the laborious operating with canonical systems in the past, where perhaps too much attention was paid to views borrowed from political society, always strove ultimately to serve the law of love, even in section 2 of Canon 81.

The Motu Proprio, mentioned above, reserves all kinds of cases to the pope in view of saving unity in important matters among the bishops of the Latin Church. This is in itself normal and healthy, on condition that such an arrangement still serves the true salvation of the faithful, which, in our understanding today, may not be identical with human happiness but is nevertheless based on it. In the past such regulations too easily showed a tendency to substitute obedience to the law for obedience to faith and love. Too often these regulations made the bishops lose sight of their personal function and their personal responsibility to the Lord. Too often did a false mystique of obedience obstruct the freedom of the children of God, not to mention an ecclesiastical policy which left people out in the cold and, under the flag of obedience to the law, shied away from the real task to make Christ's love triumph. And yet only this love can make the message credible.

Insofar as our particular subject is concerned, we have to conclude that in general the bishops are only too willing to cling to the general directives from Rome and to respect the reservation of specific cases. But this will never absolve them from their direct responsibility to the Lord. Now that what happens in the Church at the local level has become of primary importance, since it is there that the community of Christ really lives, the bishops will have to be most sensitive to the truth that the personal happiness

[25] H. J. Kemmeren, "Dispensatie," in *Catholica. Informatiebron voor het katholieke leven* (1968).

of human beings cannot be sacrificed to general rules and systems. The modern sense of living will no longer tolerate this, and the modern practice of the Gospel of love will do so still less. Therefore, if a need in the Church for dispensation ever existed, then it is surely today, when the unique and irreplaceable dignity of the human person has to be faced. The first, the last and the ultimately decisive issue for the bishop is then not what the law says, but what Christ wants. And this is reinforced by the fact that the ultimate and decisive intention of the law is precisely to provide this service. Therefore, if the bishop is of the opinion that waiting for a dispensation from Rome would do great harm to the person concerned or to others, the bishop could grant this dispensation himself.

And if we pursue these principles logically, we can even consider it at least a theoretical possibility that a bishop should not only dispense a priest from celibacy but also, against the usual practice of the Roman curia, allow him to continue in his ministry, "because otherwise the flock entrusted to him would remain without the necessary help in the case of pressing needs". [26] In practice this would hardly be necessary, since in such a pressing situation the Roman curia itself would doubtless change its practice. The point is simply the understanding of the fact that the juridical structure can never have the last word. If such a case were ever brought up, the debate should never be limited to the strictly canonical question whether or not the current system of Canon Law allows for such competence. In Church order we shall always have to remain open to the possibility that the direct obedience to Christ will suspend the normal strictures of positive law. A Church order which would exclude this possibility in principle or in practice has already excluded the Spirit of Christ as an evangelical reality. That in principle law and love cannot contradict each other in the Church means that possible contradictions must be canceled out by the overriding power of Christ.

[26] Reiffenstuel, *op. cit.*

Giovanni Řezáč, S.J./*Rome, Italy*

The Extension of the Power of the Patriarchs and of the Eastern Churches over the Faithful of Their Own Rites

In its *Decree on the Catholic Churches of the Eastern Rite,* Vatican Council II contributed greatly to the reestablishment of the dignity of Patriarchs as well as to their powers.[1] But not all that was desired has come to pass, either because the problems were possibly not yet ripe or perhaps because certain questions were for various reasons not presented for public discussion. Hence a solution was achieved which we might call interlocutorial, yielding only a partial satisfaction. Among the questions which remained suspended in this way is that of the precedence of patriarchs and that of the extension of their powers to all the faithful of their rite wherever they be—and hence even outside the patriarchates. We will deal with the second question which is of greater importance pastorally for the good of souls—a factor so greatly and so often stressed by the Council.

I

Cardinal Coussa, speaking of the jurisdiction of patriarchs over the faithful of their rite who reside outside the patriarchate, states: "It is a holy thing in the ancient canons and in the tradition of even

[1] Cf. nn. 7-11, 17, 19, 20, 23.

the Eastern Church that patriarchs and bishops *have no power
over the faithful of their rite who reside outside their own territory,* if these are not subject to them." [2] And in confirmation of
this statement he cites a letter of the Congregation for the Propagation of the Faith of May 12, 1890 to the archbishop of
Paris: "It is a general maxim of the Sacred Congregation that
the patriarchs of the Eastern Rite cannot exercise their jurisdiction
outside their patriarchate, and consequently that priests or faithful of any Eastern Rite who have a domicile outside their respective
patriarchates or *even within their limits* but do not have pastors of
their rite are subject to the Latin ordinary of the place in which
they reside, especially in Latin dioceses." [3]

The norm mentioned above, as underscored by Cardinal
Coussa, comes from the ancient tradition of the Church. It is
already indicated by Canon 6 of the First Council of Nicea
which defines the powers of the three principal bishops of that
time—namely, the bishop of Rome, of Alexandria, and of
Antioch: "Let the ancient custom be preserved in Egypt, Libya
and the Pentapolis so that the bishop of Alexandria has power
over all three regions, for this is also the custom of the bishop of
the city of Rome, and similarly in Antioch and the other provinces
let the proper privileges be preserved for the Churches." [4]

This is set forth even more clearly in Canon 2 of the First
Council of Constantinople where these supreme hierarchs are
forbidden to exercise their power beyond the confines of their own
territory: "Bishops who are over dioceses [that is, seculars] *must
not set foot in churches which are outside their confines* and not
disturb them [in any way]; rather, in accord with the canons,
*the bishops of Alexandria must administer solely Egyptian
affairs* and the bishops [of the dioceses] of the East must

---

[2] *Epitome praelectionum de iure ecclesiastico orientali,* Vol. I (Grot-
taferrata, 1948), p. 229.

[3] *Ibid.* It makes one wonder that even under Leo XIII maxims could
be enunciated which limited in this way the power of patriarchs even in
their own territory.

[4] P. P. Joannou, *Les canons des conciles oecuméniques, in Fonti* (Grot-
taferrata, 1962), pp. 28-29.

govern only over the East, observing the principles which were attributed to the Church of Antioch by the Nicene canons. And the bishops of the dioceses of Asia [i.e., Ephesus] must rule only the affairs of Asiatic dioceses, and those [of the diocese] of Pontus [i.e., Caesarea of Cappadocia] only the affairs of Pontus, and those [of the diocese] of Thrace [i.e., Heraclea] only the affairs of Thrace. Unless they are called, *bishops must not go out from their [own] diocese for elections and ordinations of bishops* or to regulate other ecclesiatical questions. Observing the above norms regarding dioceses, it is evident that according to the decisions of Nicea the provincial synod must regulate the affairs of every province." [5] Hence, every head of these territorial eccle-siastical unities, later called exarch and patriarch, is limited in the exercise of his power to his territory alone—in which, how-ever, he truly enjoys exclusive competence over all.

This is the principle of territorial power, herein defined, which remained intact for many centuries, at least as regards the delimitation of jurisdiction even with respect to patriarchs—at least in theory. However, it was in fact violated almost imme-diately. Then it was ratified with the consensus at least of one part of the fathers of the Council of Chalcedon in Canon 28, through the extension of the powers of the bishop and then the archbishop of Constantinople to the three exarchates—namely, Pontus, Asia and Thrace—and the absorption of the powers of the exarchs of Caesarea in Cappadocia, of Ephesus and of Heraclea; in addition, it was adapted to the widening of the pa-triarchate of Constantinople thus created, to mission lands such as Russia, and then extended to Bulgaria, Serbia, Rumania, etc., and in the last decades with the emigration to the Old and New World it was extended even to those points.

However, we must note that while at the beginning this in-cluded the exclusive power over all one's territory, such an exclu-sivity later on came to be ever more restricted—owing to the christological controversies and schisms produced by them, as

[5] *Ibid.*, pp. 46-47.

well as because of the Islamic invasions—in the personal sense, that is, in regard to determinate *subjects* only (the Orthodox), changing itself into the territorial-personal principle, as we see it commonly applied today both among the separated Churches and among the Catholic Church.

The whole process so far considered developed within the ambit of the Eastern Church or Churches or patriarchates. The Western Church or Roman patriarchate remains outside these events. But with the coming of the Crusaders and the founding of the Latin patriarchates and other constituencies over the territories of the Eastern Church and Eastern patriarchates, from the end of the 11th century onward, even the Latin Church became involved in the matter. As a consequence the principle of the territorial delimitation of patriarchates and the non-interference of one patriarch in the territory of the others becomes definitely surpassed.

This represented the first time that the Roman patriarchate and the Western Church was established in the territories of the Eastern patriarchates (if we prescind from brief attempts in Bulgaria and Serbia), creating the Latin patriarchates of Jerusalem (1099) and Antioch (1100). In justification of this, some could allege that the patriarchate of Constantinople had already done the same thing in the 8th century under Leo Isauricus, withdrawing Sicily, southern Italy and eastern Illyricum from the Church of Rome; moreover, possibly after 1054, since there was no longer communion even with the Churches of the Byzantine Rite, there was the necessity to provide for the spiritual needs of the Crusaders with Latin Catholic clergy. In any case, the fact of the overthrow of territorial limits even on the part of the Roman patriarchate and the Western Church with respect to these Eastern territories remained, and was actually confirmed by the 4th Crusade which resulted in the occupation of Constantinople and the creation of a Latin patriarchate even there (1204) and a bit later also in Alexandria (1209).

This state of affairs—that is, the coexistence of various Eastern Churches as well as Latin constituencies over the same territory of Eastern patriarchates—continued to remain even when parts of these Churches, especially from the 16th century onward, became united with the Apostolic See and began to constitute Eastern Catholic Churches. Thus, the norm of the territoriality of jurisdiction came—at least in these regions—to be definitely set aside, losing its universal value, and its place even in the Catholic Church was taken by the norm of the personality of jurisdiction—that is, by the persons of a certain rite or Church only, in a determinate territory, a principle already followed for centuries by the various separated Churches. In this new conception the Latin Church also found a place with all of the juridic arrangement proper to it, even though it was in a territory traditionally not its own, and even though there was little objective necessity for such an organization after the disappearance of the conquests of the Crusaders, given the scarcity of Latin faithful in the East, who were, so to speak, artificially kept alive, especially through proselytism among the Orthodox, to the great scandal of the Eastern Catholic and Orthodox Churches.

Hence, in this case the norm cited at the beginning: *"Patriarchs and bishops have no power over the faithful of their rite who reside outside their own territory,* if these are not subject to them"—although it was based on tradition and during the first millennium was observed even by the Roman patriarchate and the Latin Church—was no longer followed. In other words, it was of no further value as an obligatory norm, because "it fell into desuetude", *or* it was in the future to be understood as meaning that the confines of one's patriarchate are extended even as far as the faithful extend or at least the constituencies of one's rite.

We speak of the *Latin Church* because after the year 1000 the Roman patriarchate is almost never spoken of, but the principle remains the same. The Latin Church is in the sense of the Catholic Church only *one particular Church,* although it is the most numerous and for various reasons the most important; it is always only one particular Church *whose rights and duties* are in themselves *equal* to those of any other particular Eastern Church or rite, as it is customary to say, in the Catholic Church. This is explicitly stated by the Vatican Council II in n. 3 of the *Decree on the Catholic Churches of the Eastern Rite:* "Such *particular Churches,* whether of the *East* or of the *West,* although they differ somewhat among themselves in what are called rites (that is, in liturgy, ecclesiastical discipline, and spiritual heritage) are, nevertheless, *equally* entrusted to the pastoral guidance of the Roman Pontiff, the divinely appointed successor of St. Peter in supreme governance over the universal Church. *They are consequently* of equal dignity, so that none of them is superior to the others by reason of rite. *They enjoy the same rights and are under the same obligations,* even with respect to preaching the Gospel to the whole world (cf. Mk. 16, 15) under the guidance of the Roman Pontiff."

II

This norm of the *equality of particular Churches* with one another which in itself is clear and, I would say, evident—especially in our day—was never before expressed so forcefully. But in order that it will not remain on the purely theoretical level, all the consequences must be drawn from it. One of these, generally the most important, concerns our subject. What I mean to say is that if the Latin Church, a particular Church, can exercise its jurisdiction wherever its own subjects are located, I do not see why the same right should not be recognized, to the same extent, even for the other particular Churches, the Eastern Churches. This is not a question of prestige but simply one of justice. Otherwise, we cannot speak in the Catholic Church of the equality of rites or of particular Churches, and the statement of the Council cited above will remain solely a pious wish that does not correspond with the real state of things and does not respond simply to the truth—a conclusion which is inadmissible.

In order to explain somewhat the difficulty inherent in the integral and honest application of the enunciated principle of the equality of particular Churches, we must realize that, prescinding from the Armenians of Poland who have resided there since the 14th century and later in Transylvania, the presence of Easterners in Western regions is a relatively recent phenomenon, just anterior to the beginning of the 20th century. Until that date the Easterners continued to reside generally in Eastern regions. It was only in the closing decades of the 19th century that the first migrations were recorded, abundantly made up of Ruthenians and Ukrainians from Subcarpazia and Galizia to the United States of America, Canada, and South America. The same thing happened a bit later in the case of the Melchites and Maronites, especially from Lebanon, Syria, and Palestine, to the same regions. The other Eastern Catholics are found therein in smaller numbers and do not really constitute a serious problem.

Who is to minister ecclesiastically to all these Eastern Christians who are outside their traditional sees? There is generally no problem in the case of the Orthodox or the separated brethren. With the exception of the Greeks who in great part depend on the ecumenical patriarchate, the others at first preserved or still continue to preserve their dependence on their mother Church, since all the Churches are autocephalous as such, equal among one another. For the Eastern Catholics, however, the affair was more complicated because of the Latin hierarchy existing in those countries which was regarded as solely competent for all Catholics of whatever origin and whatever rite. To justify such an attitude one could cite the famous chapter 9 of the Fourth Lateran Council which did not admit the multiplicity of hierarchies in the same places but required only that the needs of the faithful of other rites be provided for under the name of the vicar general of such rites.[6] This norm—notwithstanding its meager efficacy

[6] This insistence on a traditional principle could have seemed strange, but it was already not in line with reality and hence anachronistic whether among the Eastern Churches or even among the Latin Church, after the introduction of the Latin hierarchy into various Eastern sees with the Crusaders. And in fact it never achieved any success; instead it was the cause of ever more difficulties when on certain occasions it was

—was out of necessity applied by Pius IX to the Armenians in Russia in the Latin dioceses of Kameneck and Chersoneso [7] and in a more general way by Leo XIII in the Constitution *Orientalium dignitas* of November 30, 1894 [8] which states: "Every Easterner residing outside the patriarchal territory should be under the administration of the Latin clergy." This was a solution corresponding to the pressing need of the moment: in the new countries of the emigrants there was no other clergy and hierarchy beside the Latin one; hence, the Eastern Catholics were subjected to it.

But it was soon realized that such a solution was neither ideal nor even merely adequate, especially because of the lack of preparation on the part of the local clergy, for whom the new emigrants posed problems that were more than they could handle. It was therefore necessary to call on the respective clergy of the faithful in question. And even with regard to the Latin hierarchy of the place, there was the same lack of preparation which, especially among the Slavs, caused massive defections and departures for the separated Churches, much better organized under this aspect.

Thus 1907 saw the naming of a Slavic bishop, first only as a vicar for Latin bishops, notwithstanding the sad experience which we have mentioned this solution had yielded in Western Europe in the past; [9] such an experience was confirmed also in this case, and hence in 1914 full jurisdiction was granted him. In 1916 two apostolic administrators were named, one for the Ukrainians stemming from Galizia, the other for the Ruthenians of Subcarpazia, with sees at Philadelphia and Pittsburgh respectively. This situation had remained unchanged for 49 years, when

---

desired to apply it, as in the first Unions in the Balkans, etc. Hence, either no vicar was granted to the Easterners, as, for example, among the Italo-Albanese and the Malabarites for a long time, or to avoid greater evils one was forced to institute an Eastern hierarchy independent of the Latin bishops; this is the only solution possible today, wherever the circumstances permit it.

[7] Cf. Allocution *Probe nostris* (1848): *Coll. Lacen.* II, n. 56, p. 557.
[8] *Collectanea S. C. de Prop. Fide* II, n. 1883.
[9] Cf., for example, Sirmium.

in 1956 a new exarchy was erected in Stamford, separated from Philadelphia and constituted as an ecclesiastical province in 1958, enriched in 1961 with another eparchy, that of St. Nicholas of Chicago. Even the exarchy of Pittsburgh was divided in 1963 and erected into an eparchy with that of Passaic, but these have remained directly subject to the Apostolic See.

An analogous development took place for the Ukrainians of Canada. In 1912 there was one ordinariate; it was divided into three exarchies in 1946 and into four in 1951, and in 1956 it was erected into an ecclesiastical province. On the other hand, in Brazil the evolution was much more gradual; only in 1951 was an ordinariate erected for all Eastern Catholics, with a Latin ordinary but with an Eastern vicar general for the Maronites, Melchites and Ukrainians; for these latter an exarchy was erected in 1962. Subsequently, exarchies were erected for the Ukrainians in England (1957), in Australia (1958), in Germany (1959) and in France (1960), and at the same time one also for the Armenians, while an ordinariate for all Eastern Catholics already existed from 1954; finally, an ordinariate was erected in Argentina (1959) equally for all Eastern Catholics, but with an apostolic visitor for the Ukrainians in 1961.

Last among these constituencies are the two exarchies in the United States of America of 1966, one for the Maronites and the other for the Melchites; their titulars are united "in the manner of suffrage" with the respective Latin sees of Detroit and Boston. The same might be said of the four exarchies erected in 1968 in Central India for the Malabarites—that of Canada, which already existed from 1962 on as an ordinariate, united with the Latin see of Nagpur, and those of Sagar, Satna, and Ujjain united with the Latin sees of Bhopal, since there was in India the proper Malabarite hierarchy. And one spontaneously asks the reason for such useless complications and anomalies. It should be noted that all these constituencies—whose erection is doubtless a great good but also a right insofar as the Eastern faithful have the right to be governed by the hierarchy of their rites—have no juridical connection at all with the rest of the hierarchy of their Church, which certainly would not favor the ordered development of the individual Churches in question.

III

It seems that the moment has now arrived for this dolorous problem to be resolved in a definitive manner, according to the nature of things. Here are a few reasons:

1. We have seen above that the *equality of rights* among particular Churches solemnly proclaimed by Vatican Council II requires that even the Eastern Churches can exercise their jurisdiction over the faithful of their own rite everywhere, as the Latin Church has done for centuries.

2. The Eastern Churches—which already seem to possess the quasi-natural right of all mother Churches regarding the care of the faithful of their own rite wherever they might be—are also *those most* fitted to exercise it, either because of their own interests not to lose these faithful and so diminish numerically and in other respects, or because they are better prepared for such a task. On the other hand, the local clergy either are not greatly interested in these particular faithful since they are foreigners— and so much the less if they are Easterners—or even if they desire to be interested they are not sufficiently prepared to be able to exercise such care with real profit. Hence, it seems that such care should be entrusted to those who are more capable and more truly interested in exercising it for the good of souls.

3. *The principle of subsidiarity* enunciated by Pius XI with respect to social teaching, but which has universal value, finds application even in our question: *"Since it is illicit* to deprive any individuals of what they can accomplish with their own powers and proper industry in order to hand it over to the community, so is it to remit to a higher and more elevated society *that which can be done by smaller and lower communities.* And this is both a *grave danger* and a *disturbance of the right order of society."* [10]

[10] Encyclical *Quadragesimo anno,* (1931): *AAS* 23 (1931), p. 203.

Then Pius XII in the allocution to the cardinals of February 20, 1946 emphasized that such a norm was valid even for the Church: "These are words that are truly luminous and *hold good* for the social life in all its phases, and even for the *life of the Church, without prejudice to its hierarchical structure.*" [11] Hence, according to this principle, anything that a particular Eastern Church and its bishops can do should not be reserved to or impeded by the superior or supreme power—namely, the question before us; the care of the faithful of one's own rite should be per se entrusted to the Church of the rite in question: otherwise, we run the risk of disturbing the right order of things.

4. The *personal character of ecclesiastical society* demands the same thing. The Church is a society of the baptized, hence of men united to it by a personal bond, which is baptism, prescinding from the place in which they might be; the territorial element does not enter into its definition as it does, however, in the definition of the State. Thus there is no obstacle in the fact that in a territory there are several particular Churches, since even these Churches have the personal character insofar as they unite the faithful of the same rite—that is, those who were baptized in the same rite or should have been, or have adhered to it with due permission. This personal character of ecclesiastical society is nowadays confirmed by the definition of a diocese given by the Council: "*A diocese is that portion of God's people* which is entrusted to a bishop to be shepherded by him with the cooperation of the presbytery. Adhering thus to its pastor . . . this portion constitutes a particular Church." [12] Note that there is no mention at all of territory, which is accordingly not in the least essential.

5. This is demanded, in particular, *as regards the patriarchs themselves.* We prescind from the argument from equality which is clearer when applied to the particular Churches than to patriarchs, since in the person of the Roman pontiff the person

[11] Cf. *AAS* 38 (1946), p. 145.

[12] Cf. the *Decree on the Pastoral Office of Bishops in the Church*, n. 11. Here the term "particular Church" is used in another sense than the one used by us in the article—that is, it signifies dioceses.

of the patriarch of the West is always united to the person of the head of the universal Church, and—especially today but even from the first centuries of the second millennium—is consequently placed on the second level and absorbed so that one no longer speaks of him as the patriarch of the West except in an historical sense. However, in the *munus* of the patriarchs there are some aspects which require, in a more particular way, the extension of their powers to all the faithful of their rite even if these reside outside their patriarchate:

(a) First of all this is deduced from the very *notion of patriarch,* as head of a particular Church or rite, which requires that his power extend over all the faithful of such a Church, whether inside or outside the patriarchate. Otherwise it makes no sense to speak of him as a head; at most, he would be a symbolic head. This affirmation is confirmed in a certain sense by n. 7 of the *Decree on the Catholic Churches of the Eastern Rite* which states that the patriarchs possess jurisdiction over all bishops—not excepting metropolitans—clergy and people *of their own* territory *or rite.* The first part, "of their own territory", is traditional; however, the addition of "or rite" seems to show a desire to say more—that is, of the entire rite or of all those pertaining to that rite, correcting the expression of Canon 216 which speaks of one's own territory or *rite,* in the restrictive sense, as of something that is identical. Unfortunately, even in the case before us, the words "in accordance with the norm of law" [13] are added, thus destroying the wider notion first insinuated.

The following clause of n. 7 of the Decree states: "Wherever the ordinary of any rite is appointed outside the territorial bounds of its patriarchate, he remains *attached to the hierarchy of the patriarchate* of that rite, in accordance with the norm of law." This seems to manifest the will to extend the powers of patriarchs even to these bishops but without determining anything in the concrete; in other words, it is a norm that necessarily needs to be completed.

(b) This is demanded by the Motu Proprio *Cleri.* Canon 216

[13] Cf. c. 240 of the Motu Proprio *Cleri.*

states that the patriarch possesses power over the faithful of the same rite who reside outside the limits of his territory, inasmuch as it is *expressly* stated by common or particular law. Here rite is understood in its natural extension—that is, insofar as it includes all who pertain to such a rite. It is not clear to me what particular law determines about such a power, but it is probably not a great deal; common law, on the other hand, does deal with it but in a rather contradictory fashion. Thus, for example, the Motu Proprio *Cleri* requires that patriarchs "most diligently *procure the faithful preservation and accurate observance of their rite* and neither permit nor tolerate the introduction of any change in the rite". But how can they do so if a true power over these faithful is not recognized in their case? If something serious is asked of the patriarchs, in such a case they must have the corresponding power, since duties must bear with them the corresponding powers; [14] the least that can be said here is that we are dealing with a real *lacuna iuris* which must of necessity be completed. This is confirmed even by Cardinal Coussa when speaking on the subject: "The same Sacred Congregation for the Propagation of the Faith in the past and the Sacred Congregation for the Eastern Churches today recognize the power of patriarchs over the faithful who reside outside their patriarchate—*but only in regard to rite*. Patriarchs are held to communicate to priests who exercise the care of souls the norms and decisions regarding rite. But the *manner* in which patriarchs can *effectively* exercise their vigilance over the rite *is not determined at all*. Neither is anything found concerning the co-active power of patriarchs in this regard." [15]

(c) This is demanded every day, more than anything else, by *ecumenical reasons*. It is futile to have illusions about the progress of the rapprochement with the Eastern Churches if the patriarchal dignity in the Catholic Church is not restored in its

---

[14] Cf., for example, what Canon 200 of the CIC tells us about delegated power: "It is understood that whoever receives a delegated power also is granted everything else without which that power could not be exercised."

[15] *Epitome I*, 229-230.

just rights and privileges which belong to the heads of particular Churches and which they generally enjoy now, as first in dignity, with ample powers over their faithful. In n. 9 of the *Decree on the Catholic Churches of the Eastern Rite,* Vatican Council II did much in this respect; there only remains—besides the question of precedence which is already partly resolved—the present question of the extension of jurisdiction over all the faithful of their rite, as real heads of a particular Church. No patriarch who has an accurate concept of his dignity could ever renounce it; it would be for him a real *diminutio capitis,* which neither he nor his bishops, clergy or faithful can admit. This will show the sincerity of the ecumenical will of the Catholic Church, if for the good of souls it is ready to lay aside this norm of its right which we have seen above is already anachronistic and does not respond any longer to the reality of things or to the interests of the Church itself.

(d) In addition, this is demanded by *the principle of collegiality,* by reason of which so many institutions have been revised and so many powers restored either to the bishops or to episcopal conferences; this should also counsel a rethinking and rectification of the problem treated, corroborated in such a solution by the principle of subsidiarity adopted above.

(e) Finally, this is demanded *by the necessity for overcoming the opposed difficulties* which are more apparent than real, and in any case exaggerated. The problem of the Eastern faithful in Western regions exists, and it will perhaps increase; it is therefore necessary to resolve it, and in an equitable fashion. And it must be acknowledged that much has already been done in this sense; there only remains to eliminate the other obstacles to an honorable and fraternal solution, which is also just and ecumenical and required for the good of souls. I said that the difficulties are exaggerated; in fact, it is a question in practice of only three patriarchs and a major archbishop—namely, the Armenians in Europe, the Maronites and Melchites principally in the Americas, and in addition the Ukrainians in Australia—and hence only four Churches which have more massive emigrations especially in three countries: the United States of America, Brazil and Argentina. In the United States the affair is almost resolved; as far as Brazil is concerned, there remains the erection of an exarchy for the Maronites and another for the Melchites, and the same goes for Argentina where an exarchy is also necessary for the Ukrainians who have only an apostolic visitor.

In addition, the exarchs or bishops created should be juridically bound together and would thus form part of the hierarchy of the Churches of their own rite with all their rights and duties; hence, even their election would take place in the manner of the other bishops, possibly including particular requisites, given the different circumstances. The faithful of the other rites could be entrusted to the administration of the Eastern hierarchy of those countries in accord with a mutual agreement. The Eastern bishops in the different countries could then form a kind of inter-territorial episcopal conference for the solution of mutual problems.

When seen at close range, this whole question of the extension of the powers of patriarchs or particular Churches in general to all the faithful of their own rite will appear capable of receiving an easier solution, since for many Churches it will be a question of a possibility that is more theoretical than practical. In any case, it is seemingly the only solution which can satisfy both Catholic and Orthodox Easterners and lead to a sincere and fraternal collaboration without reticence with the Latin clergy and hierarchy; it may also more effectively assure the good of the souls of the Eastern faithful and possibly even many of the Latin faithful—and hence the real good of the universal Church.

Andrew Greeley/*Chicago, Illinois*

Canon Law and Society

Every human community is held together by a common set of values. Some of these values prescribe the behavior that is expected of members of the community and are called "norms" by the sociologist. Some of the norms are of such importance that they are codified and enforced by those who have the power in the community. Such forms of norms imposed by those in authority are called "laws", and every human community (beyond simple relationships in family and friendship groups) is governed by some sort of law.

Law and Society

The relationship between law and society is ambiguous, for the society. The Anglo-Saxon common law in Great Britain and the United States, for example, is rooted deep in the past of the common culture from which these two societies spring; while the experience of the English-speaking countries has modified, revised and developed the common law tradition, similarly the tradition itself has given direction and form to the experience of the English-speaking societies.

Law, if it is to be effective, must be both conservative and liberal—conservative so that it preserves the traditions in which the society is founded, and liberal so that it is flexible enough for these traditions to be able to develop to meet changing circumstances in which the society finds itself. The worn thing that can happen to a legal system is for it to become socially irrelevant, for then it no longer conserves the tradition over which it has been given charge, nor does it enable that tradition to be open enough to grow and change to meet the new challenges of changing circumstances. A legal system that has lost contact with the social reality in which those for whom it is intended live simultaneously produces a "normless" society and acts as a tyrant, for it does not offer a form of norms that are relevant to the situation in which people find themselves, and also imposes norms which have long since become irrelevant.

Canon Law and Church

The Canon Law tradition is a great and noble one, and its most recent codification in the 1919 Code of Canon Law was unquestionably a work of extraordinarily skilled jurists, yet the sociologist who assays the empirical evidence is forced to conclude that Canon Law *in its present form* has become largely irrelevant for most Catholics. Large numbers of clergy and probably the majority of Catholic laity are in the process of withdrawing their consensus from major sections of Canon Law, and it would appear that no amount of threats about canonical punishments will be able to reverse the trend. There are many reasons for this withdrawal of consensus. Poor administration is certainly one of them; for example, the long wait to obtain decision in marriage cases and the atrophying of the appelate processes seem to have turned many against the canonical system. Furthermore, the implicit assumption of Canon Law—namely, that the Church is a State within a State—may have been quite pertinent in the Middle Ages, and even the Renaissance, but it is archaic today and creates an atmosphere of strangeness about Canon Law which makes many educated Catholics feel that it is just a bit quaint. However, both of these two weaknesses could be corrected and still the basic problem with the existing Code of Canon Law would remain: it is a legal system which no longer corresponds to social reality.

For What Kind of Society?

It is instructive to read through the Code and the many interpretations that have been rendered concerning it, and then to ask oneself what kind of society it seems to assume. With some minor exceptions, the Code of Canon Law seems to imagine a world which might have existed in late 18th-century Western Europe.

First of all, the Code does not seem to be aware that there are large cities; there are vicars *foraine* (C445-449) referred to, but no vicars *urbaine*. The parish priest (C451-465) is the object of much legislation, but his *cooperator* (C476) is barely mentioned. It is therefore assumed that most parishes are small parishes in small towns, tended by one priest, with an occasional parish having a young man who assists the pastor for a time before he becomes a pastor himself. The large city parish with many priests and thousands of people is beyond the purview of the Code.

It is also generally assumed that everyone in the parish knows everyone else, and that the reading of the banns of matrimony will therefore be a guarantee that no one will be able to engage in deceit when they are planning marriage (C1022). Transportation and communication are likewise assumed to be rather slow. The Code does not know of the telephone and presumes that there are many sets of circumstances in which the parish priest cannot be in immediate touch with his bishop (C1045-1046); it also assumes a highly stable population with the *vagus* and the *peregrinus* (C91) being rather unusual creatures whom one would seldom encounter. The parish in which one is baptized is therefore considered to be the parish *par excellence* for the rest of one's life. And here one must go to find one's essential ecclesiastical record (C777-779).

The parish priest in his parish and the bishop in his diocese have great powers, both because the decisions they must make are presumed to be relevantly simple and because neither their *cooperators* nor the laity are able to add much to the knowledge and the insight that the pastor and the bishop already possess in abundance.

Women are definitely inferior beings. Whatever power conceded to them is second-rate power, and they are expected to look to men for ultimate decisions. The Code is careful to protect their rights, but nevertheless these rights are simply not comparable with the rights that the male leadership possesses. For example, she cannot speak for herself during a canonizational process, a rule that applies also to children and imbeciles (C2004).

Furthermore, the Code presumes that one obtains consent to laws basically by the threat of punishment, and it makes available to ecclesiastical authority a wide variety of penalties which one suspects must cause wry amusement among those non-Catholic scholars who study the canonical system of penalties; a system which may have been useful in the Middle Ages has precious little to do either with the reality of the Church's power in the 20th century or, for that matter, the spirit of the Gospel (C2193-2241).

While there are provisions in the Code, as there must be in every legal system, for the right of appeal, Canon Law is not nearly as sensitive as are most other modern legal systems to due process, a separation of the judiciary from the executive, and the civil rights and liberties of individual citizens. Canonical processes and protections would compare favorably, one imagines, with legal procedures perhaps even in the middle of the 19th century, but compared with, let us say, the protection of individual freedom provided by the Supreme Court of the United States under Chief Justice Earl Warren, the Code's concern with civil liberties seems rather primitive.

One would also look in vain in the Code or the interpretations or decisions on it to find much in the way of psychological or sociological sophistication. The possibility that a marriage could be declared null because one of the contracting partners had a psychopathic personality is hailed as a major breakthrough in canonical decisions, when, in fact, our knowledge of the human personality in society is advanced far beyond the realization that the psychopath cannot make a valid commitment. Even the McNaughton rule, which is under heavy fire in Anglo-Saxon civil law, is far more generous in its interpretation of legal insanity than is the Code. One has the impression from the canonical discussions of the nature of the marriage contract that the two partners who agree to this very rational contract are Adam Smith's economic man and his wife, and they surely do not have any of the dimensions of the personality of which Sigmund Freud wrote. Nor, would it seem, are they affected by such things as social class, ethnicity or cultural origins.

Finally, the Code seems to assume a world in which long-range decisions are possible—that is, a world where change, both in the individual and in society, is relatively slow. Therefore there is no need for short-range decisions which can be modified or changed to respond to changing circumstances.

The World Has Changed

The defenders of the Code of Canon Law may argue that this is an unduly harsh description of it, and that in practice many modifications and interpretations can take place which make the system more modern than it might appear. Surely any legal system can be stretched and twisted to fit a different set of circumstances than that for which it was initially written. The Constitution of the United States, for example, has evolved a long way from the society of yeoman farmers for which it was originally written, but a brief constitution evolves much more easily than does a system of more than 2,000 regulations, and the present system, whatever its unquestioned merits, does not correspond to the world in which most Catholics live. It is irrelevant to them.

First of all, the world has become urban. Not merely in the North Atlantic countries, but also in the emerging nations of Asia, Africa and South America, the population is rapidly concentrating in large cities. Teams of priests working together on a collegial and cooperative basis, sharing their highly developed professional specialties, are the only ministry in which the Church can expect to cope with urban problems, and yet the traditional territorial parish with its traditional authoritarian pastor remains the canonical model for the Christian community.

In addition to being an urban society, it is also a world society. Canon Law, Roman in its origins and roots, may still be intelligible to the Western European mind, but it is understood only with very great difficulty by the Japanese or Indian mind, and presumably makes no sense at all to the African. It can, one imagines, be translated into Swahili, and even described in categories that may be meaningful to those who speak Swahili, but one suspects that such ideas as the excommunication *vitandus* seem as quaint to the Swahili as does the idea that Jacqueline Kennedy is a public sinner seems quaint to Americans.

It is furthermore a world of instant communication and almost instant transportation. There are few places in the world that are further away than the flick of a finger on one's telephone, and almost no place in the world that cannot be reached in less than 24 hours from any other place in the world. Not only the human voice but written documents may be transmitted instantaneously to any part of the globe. The fact that canonical regulations and procedures do not take this instant communication and almost instant transportation for granted may be relatively minor compared to the mistake of imposing rural parishes on urban settings, or Roman regulations on the Swahili and the Japanese, but it does indicate that Canon Law, in its attempt to be timeless, has succeeded only in being dated, and in its attempt to be applicable to almost all situations it has succeeded in being relevant to almost none.

Furthermore, particularly in the North Atlantic countries the Catholic population is no longer made up of simple uneducated peasants who look to their clergy for leadership and for wise prudent decisions. On the contrary, in most countries the practicing Catholic population is made up largely of well-educated professionals who are used to being treated as mature adults in the world of their occupation and are very ill at ease to discover that the Church views them pretty much as legal infants.

In the modern world, decisions, at least the critical decisions made in the important decision-making posts, are not rendered by one man, but rather by teams of skilled experts who bring vastly diverse training, competencies, insights and information to the decision-making process. The response of President Kennedy and his staff to the Cuban missile crisis was necessarily a collegial one, because no single person could be expected to have the information and the insights and skills to cope with such a situation. Unilateral decision-making is as outmoded in the Church as it is in the civil society for purely pragmatic reasons: it does not work. Collegiality is no longer an option, and its necessity is rooted not so much in ethical or philosophical considerations, but rather in sheer pragmatic effectiveness.

The modern world has progressed a long way since Thomas Jefferson's Bill of Rights, the North Atlantic community has evolved at a rapidly accelerating pace, with a passion for human rights and liberties. A legal system which does not lean over backward to protect the individual from being abused by large corporate bodies is a legal system that will be judged by modern man as being morally disreputable.

The modern world has by no means rejected the idea that laws exist to bind society together, nor can it legitimately claim as its unique discovery the concept that the law must be the defender of persons. However, the defense of the person, his dignity and freedom, his right to develop his own talents, has assumed in the modern age an importance that it lacked in years gone by. While the equality of women before the law is not yet adequately guaranteed in Western societies, and is only beginning to be understood in non-Western societies, it is nonetheless a matter of central concern in the modern world. No legal system which is not evolving toward equal rights for women will earn respect from sophisticated, contemporary thinkers.

Reform of Canon Law?

Canon Law, then, is trying to cope with a society that is both urban and worldwide, held together by instant communication and almost instant transportation, peopled by citizens who are increasingly well-educated professionals; a society with a great deal of sophistication about the complexities of the human personality and human interaction patterns and with a passion for human rights, civil liberties and equality for women; a society where the uniqueness of the individual person is of paramount importance; and, finally, a society where decisions are necessarily collegial, if they are to be effective. It is no exaggeration to say that the Code of Canon Law as it presently exists is viewed by men of this modern society as something curiously foreign and outmoded. Even within the Church it has relatively few defenders, save for those professional canonists whose training and practice has blinded them to any realities beyond their textbooks. But it would seem that even the majority of those who have been trained in Canon Law, even though they are not adequately represented on the Commission for the Revision of the Code, are fully aware of the weaknesses of the legal instrument for which they have been trained. The most vigorous of those agitating for the reform of Canon Law are themselves canon lawyers.

One might well ask what happened to what was basically a sound and even brilliant legal system. While the total answer to such a question is complex, the central weakness of the canonical tradition is simple enough: it could not change as readily as was necessary, and it did not change very much at all. One could argue that the Anglo-Saxon juridic tradition with its emphasis on the empirical approach to law was more suited for a dynamic world than was the more *a priori* Roman approach to law. Certainly most Americans and Englishmen feel that common law is much more flexible and dynamic than the canonical tradition. The present writer is not qualified, however, to evaluate such a judgment. Surely the legal systems of France and Italy, for example, have proven reasonably flexible in the face of a rapidly changing world. Furthermore, the common law tradition is filled with archaic notions, some of which are positively harmful to society.[1] The failure of the Code to evolve more rapidly is not to be attributed to the fact that it is Roman law, but rather to the fact that it is Roman Catholic law, and that the Roman Catholic Church in the Counter-Reformation era was vigorously pursuing a policy of refusing to change at all. Canon Law was simultaneously the result of this policy and the means for continuing it. The policy came to an end with Vatican Council II, but the present system of Canon Law continues, a relic of the past and an impediment to the implementation of the new policies of the Church.

Can the canonical tradition be restored and made vigorous again? The only answer that must be given to that question is: Of course it can. It has been rejuvenated in the past and there is no reason why it cannot be rejuvenated again. Whether at present it will, in fact, be restored remains to be seen. Many observers are quite pessimistic about the work of the commission that is revising the code; no one doubts that there will be some change and some modernization, but whether it will be radical enough to arrest a withdrawal of consent from Canon Law remains to be seen.

How the Canonical Tradition Can Be Rejuvenated

The sociological observer would note that the following reforms seem almost essential:

1. Canon Law must contain a bill of rights—an enumeration of the rights of all Christians against the organized Church which no man, pope, bishop or priest may violate. To argue that no one needs to have such a bill of rights against the Church because the Church is Christ's community is to ignore the obvious fact

---

[1] For example, the practice of "contract buying" of houses in the United States which has been used as a tool for exploiting the poor blacks.

that for 2,000 years churchmen have frequently used their position to oppress those given to their charge. One must remember that the Lord was very harsh on the scribes and the Pharisees.

2. It must be insisted that all Christians share equality before the law, be they men or women, young or old, priests or laymen, bishops or associate pastors. No man must be permitted to use his position to interfere with the rights and freedoms of any other man.

3. Collegiality must be institutionalized in the legal system so that governance by corporate decision-making, instead of by unilateral decision-making, be reinforced by the law, instead of having it take place despite the law.

4. The right to due process of the law must be zealously safeguarded. The right to counsel, to confront one's accusers, to cross-examine, to a speedy hearing, to appeal to an impartial higher court, must be zealously safeguarded. The Church can no longer tolerate a situation where the same body of men can play the role of prosecuting attorney, judge, jury, appelate court, and, if needs be, executioner.

5. There must be more concern for the dignity and freedom of the person. The modern world will find it very difficult to understand why a sacrament is more important than a person, just as many Catholics find it extremely difficult to understand why canonical processes seem to be so much less sensitive to human needs and problems than do civil processes.

6. In all likelihood the office of ombudsman must be established in the Church (presumably the office of a tribune is not entirely unknown in the Roman legal system) to ensure that a hasty redress of grievance is available to the individual Christian in such circumstances when he seems to be the victim of an unjust or inequitable action on the part of someone in a higher position.

7. The universal law of the Church probably should be very simple—indeed, little more than a constitution laying down basic rights, principles and themes. Perhaps it was possible to

legislate for the *orbis terrarum* when the world was little more than Western Europe, but it is surely impossible today, and therefore it seems evident that the national conferences of bishops must be empowered to legislate for their own countries, with Rome serving principally in the role of an appelate jurisdiction.

8. There must also be built into the canonical system mechanisms for communication, self-criticism and accountability. Documents of Vatican Council II presume that institutions will come into existence to serve these purposes, but while some progress has been made toward the creation of such institutions since the end of the Council, the progress has not kept pace with the need for such institutions, or indeed with the demand for them.

9. The whole bizarre, archaic system of censures should be thrown bodily into the Tiber River. It may be necessary for the Church to declare that someone has behaved in such a fashion that it is impossible to see how he can any longer consider himself a member of the Christian community, but beyond that, the system of censures is a scandal to most non-Catholics and a mystery to most Catholics. Furthermore, it is almost completely unenforceable. It also may be necessary to specify procedures whereby various religious functionaries may be removed from their jobs, but such decisions should only take place after due process, and should much more profitably be called "dismissals" or "retirements" than "suspensions".

10. The censorship of books, one of the most annoying, maddening and insulting aspects of the present Code, should be similarly committed to the waters of the Tiber, along with prohibition against the reading of books. By this point the Catholic Church should have learned that she cannot fight the printing press, and that the surest way to make a book popular is to tell people that they cannot read it. Furthermore, if a scholar's writings are in theological error, condemnation will be far more effective if it is made by his professional colleagues in their critical reviews than if it is made by a seminary professor who has never written a book in his life and whose knowledge of theology

is limited to pre-1935 manuals on which his lecture notes are based. Censorship does not work; it is frequently unfair and more frequently inept; it disgusts Catholics and repels non-Catholics, and the sooner Catholicism can forget about it, the better.

11. Finally, if there is to be marriage legislation in the new Code—and there is apparently considerable controversy as to whether a legal approach to marriage problems is appropriate for the Church—then surely the Code should display much greater awareness of the sociological and psychological context of marriage. As a matter of fact, it should be possible for Church law here to show the way to civil law by being far more sensitive to the complexities of the human personality.

There are those who would argue that there should be no law in the Church—that the People of God are governed by an authority which is different from all human authority, which should need no law to maintain order within its community. We are told that authority of the Church is authority of love and service and hence different from all human authority. Sociologists must remark that these arguments are naive; in the modern world all authority justifies itself as being an authority of service, and in any human group, regulations, formal norms, established procedures, protection of rights and methods for settling disputes are essential. The Church, then, must have some law, but a more valid case could be made, it seems to the present writer, that the Church could do with much less law than it presently has. Canon Law could remain inflexible because it attempted to be so specific, and canonists could become so powerful because the very specificity of the law almost changed the Church from an organization which had laws to a legal institution in which law came to be the only unifying force. But this is too heavy a demand to make of any legal system. A law may embody the formalized norms of a culture, but it cannot by itself hold a culture together unless there is consensus about broader values and commitments to the goals inherent in these values. Perhaps the greatest mistake made by the canonical tradition in the last several centuries was to overlook this fact, and to think that in times of crisis (such as the Reformation was deemed to be) it was possible to hold the Church together by law and almost by nothing else. Even the great canonists of the Middle Ages were far more sophisticated than that; the purely juridical approach to the Church and the use of authority in the Church is a modern development (by modern we mean post-Reformation).

Paradoxically enough, even though the Code is technically unaware of the modern means of transportation and communication, it is nonetheless these modern advances that have made possible for the first time attempts at worldwide enforcement of rigid and unnuanced applications of Canon Law. For example, in the days when it took months and even years for messages to come from Rome to the United States, juridicism could not dominate the life of the American Church; the early bishops of the country were forced to apply the principles of Canon Law to their own circumstances with imagination and creativity. But now when Rome is closer to Washington than Washington was to Baltimore at the time of Archbishop John Carroll, it is possible to insist that the Roman interpretation of Canon Law can be enforced rigidly and to the letter, such uniquely American events as, for example, the case of the Sisters of the Immaculate Heart of Los Angeles.[2]

It would take someone with more historical competence than the present writer has to assert whether there has ever been a time in the past history of the Church when the Church has had too much law. But if by too much law one means law that is irrelevant, law that is needlessly detailed, law that is not truly concerned for the dignity of the individual person, then it is very easy to conclude that at the present time the Church has too much law. Either she will develop a new law that is both less extensive and more sophisticated, or she will find herself, for all practical purposes, having no law at all.

[2] Fortunately, the American hierarchy, true to the spirit of John Carroll, resisted such a blunder.

PART II
BIBLIOGRAPHICAL
SURVEY

Ivan Zužek, S.J./*Rome, Italy*

A Code for the Orthodox Churches

Orthodox is the term now used for all Oriental non-Catholic Christians. The Copts in Egypt, Ethiopians, Armenians, and other Christians, who do not recognize more than the first three ecumenical councils, are called pre-Chalcedonian Orthodox, since they officially reject the christology defined at the fourth ecumenical council held in Chalcedon in 451. However, in this article the term "Orthodox" is restricted to its more usual meaning, misleading though it may be, which designates those churches that recogize the first seven ecumenical councils, and no other. They are also called Byzantine Churches.

The Autonomy of Orthodox Churches

These churches are autocephalous—that is, independent of one another as far as the administrative authority is concerned. True, there is no general agreement as to the exact limit of this independence, but all seem to admit two distinguishing marks for an autocephalous church: (a) the right to resolve all internal problems on her own authority, and (b) the right to appoint her own bishops, including the head of the church.[1]

The right to self-government must be conceded by the mother church—that is, by the church of which the newly established

[1] Cf. A. Bogolepov, "Conditions of Autocephaly," in *St. Vladimir's Seminary Quarterly* 3 (1961), pp. 11-37.

autocephalous church was formerly a part. However, the mother-daughter relationship never actually exists, neither prior to independence, nor afterward. Once autocephalous, the church is called a "sister" with equal rights, except for honorary precedence.

Usually the mother church shows great reluctance in conceding an autocephalous status to any area under her jurisdiction. This attitude often results in a unilateral declaration of independence and long years of excommunication before the mother church finally grants official recognition to the new sister church.

The principle of autocephality is based on the 34th Canon of the Holy Apostles, which says that the bishops of every *nation* (nobody knows how to interpret this)[2] must acknowledge one bishop as chief among them, and on the 17th Canon of Chalcedon and the 38th Canon of the Council of Trullo, both of which stress that the ecclesiastical administrative structure should correspond to the political.

There are fifteen Orthodox churches canonically recognized as autocephalous: nine patriarchates (Constantinople, Alexandria, Antioch, Jerusalem, Bulgaria, Serbia, Russia, Rumania, Georgia), three "archiepiscopal churches" (Cyprus, Greece, Finland), and three "metropolitan churches" (Albania, Poland, Czechoslovakia). Only these fifteen churches have been convoked to the Pan-Orthodox meetings of recent years. Other churches, such as the Macedonian Church, the Orthodox Church in France, or the Russian-American Church, are not yet recognized as autocephalous.

None of the fifteen churches, according to a prevailing opinion of Orthodox authors, can be called *the* Orthodox Church. All sister churches as a whole, however, form the one, holy, universal and apostolic Church. None is superior to another. The ecumenical patriarch is *primus inter pares*—that is, he is given the first place in honorific precedence. Their unity is constituted by the common possession of the same Creed, the same basic traditions

[2] Cf. I. Žužek, "The Determining Structure of the Slavic *Syntagma of Fifty Titles*," in *Orientalia Christiana Periodica* 33 (1967), p.152.

and canonical order of the first eight centuries, the same liturgy, and a hierarchy of undisputed apostolic origin. As for a visible supreme authority in the Church, they are "conciliarists" in the strictest sense.

The Changing of Ancient Canons

For them, an ecumenical council is the only authority able to define dogmas and impose on all churches obligatory disciplinary prescriptions, abrogating or changing the canons of the preceding councils, or forming new ones more adapted to modern times. The impact of this principle on Orthodox Canon Law is profound: salutary, on the one hand, since it constitutes a unifying bond among the sister churches, who are bound by the same canons, but unfortunate, on the other hand, since almost every needed *aggiornamento* that the Orthodox have introduced within the last century or would like to introduce conflicts with one or another of the canons recognized as obligatory by the sixth ecumenical council, that of Trullo or *Quinisextum* of 691-692.

The necessity of changing the Common Code as promulgated by the Council of Trullo in its second canon is strongly felt by the Orthodox. A year ago [3] I quoted a few Orthodox authors who seem best to express the prevailing opinion that the doctrine of the immutablitiy of the canons "represents the rejection of a creative attitude toward contemporary life", as Afanasiev puts it. The Orthodox know that their church is a living church, belonging to this modern world, which has long ago outgrown the conditions of the first seven centuries that are reflected by the Common Code, both in its substance and in all its details. This is not to say that an "ancient canon" cannot sometimes still be the "best rule" for our times, yet the prevailing opinion does hold, again with Afanasiev, that the majority of ancient canons "can no longer be applied to modern church life in their literal sense". Many of

[3] Cf. I Zužek, "The Sacramental Canon Law of the Christian East," in *Concilium* 38 (1968), pp. 146-60; N. Afanasiev, "The Canons of the Church: Changeable or Unchangeable?" in *St. Vladimir's Seminary Quarterly* 2 (1967), pp. 54-58.

them are unnecessary, repetitious, confusing, archaic, even contradictory, and, at times, outright hindrances to the salvation of
souls.

What, for instance, is one to make of the 11th Canon of Trullo,
which forbids, under excommunication, to take medicine from
Jews or "in any way to become familiar with them"? What about
canons which prohibit "taking interest on money" (10 Trullo,
44 Apostolic Canon) or those which exclude from communion
spouses who make use of their marital rights on the same day and
all women who are menstruating (cc. 5, 6, 7, 13 of Gregory of
Nyssa)? How is one to reconcile contradictory canons? One
canon, for instance, obliges the violator of a virgin to marry her
(67 Apostolic Canon), while another solemnly declares that
"fornication is neither marriage nor the beginning of it" and,
therefore, that "it is best to separate persons joined in concubi-
nage" (26 St. Basil). There is little sense today in stressing that no
bishop should visit a military camp (the only place where the
emperor could be found) except "those whom our most reverend
emperor thinks fit to summon" (7 Sardica), or in declaring that
a certain Eutychianus or Musaeus should or should not have the
title of bishop (18 Sardica). Alivisatos notes [4] that for the same
crime certain canons prescribe most severe punishments, while
others may be interpreted in such a way that the culprit turns
out to be completely guiltless. The ancient canons on schismatics,
heretics and intercommunion would render, if applied, participation in the ecumenical movement quite impossible, whereas the
numerous ancient laws on fasting and penance, or the canons that
forbid women to paint their faces or cut their hair (17 Gangra)
and the like would render life impossible.

These few instances and what was said above make it understandable why the Orthodox hierarchy applies to many canons
the so-called "economical interpretation". In actual fact, no one
knows what economy [5] is, but it permits the bishops to maintain

[4] H. Alivisatos, "He kodikopoiesis ton hieron kanonen kai he semasia
auton," in *Epistemonike Epeteris Theologikes Scholes Panepistemiou
Anthenon* (1937), p. 57.
[5] Cf. I Zužek, *art. cit.*

the official validity of the canons and or their immutability, and, at the same time, to do without them in their actual administration of the church. There are no set rules for the use of *economy*. The determination whether an ancient canon is profitable or not for the salvation of souls (if not, one is dispensed by *economy*) is left to each individual church and, very often, to the good sense of individual bishops. Unfortunately, this "good sense" has not prevented distressing differences among the churches in their application of *economy*, which, in turn, tend to create a mistrust of the hierarchy, a disrespect for the holy canons in general, and, at times, especially with modern youth, an outright refusal to accept anything as immutable, be they canons or even dogmas.

The Possibility of a New Code

A new Common Code for all the Orthodox Churches, purged of all anient canons which are inapplicable to modern life, appears in the light of what has been said as the only solution to such problems. Of course, the purge would be only a small portion of the work required for the composition of a new Code, which would have to contain many new canons that would safeguard dogmatic, liturgical, and disciplinary unity among the Byzantine Orthodox churches.

According to Agourides, [6] Orthodoxy is, for some, "nothing more than a *koinonia latreias*", a "communion of worship", which "raises man from earth to heaven in an atmosphere of mystical exaltation". If this be the case, Orthodoxy would, of course, have little need of a common law. Some Orthodox thinkers, indeed, coming close to such an anti-legalistic view, not only deny the possibility of a common Code for Orthodoxy, but also maintain that such a Code would present that unification of the discipline of local churches which is "contrary to the Orthodox spirit," as Evdokimov puts it.[7] In a recent, highly interesting doctoral dis-

[6] S. Agourides, "The Social Character of Orthodoxy," in *The Orthodox Ethos*, ed. by A. Philippou (Oxford, 1964), pp. 210-11.
[7] P. Evdokimov, *L'Orthodoxie* (Neuchâtel-Paris, 1959), p. 183.

sertation (to which I am much indebted in writing this article), B. Archondonis,[8] in classifying the opinions of Orthodox writers about a Common Code, reserves to such authors the last place. Actually, they are very few.

Christophilopoulos [9] represents the opinion that a unique Code for Orthodoxy, though not contrary to any "spirit", is, nevertheless, impossible because of the autocephalous character of each national church. For Christophilopoulos, these churches represent, so it appears, a sort of *Kirchenbund,* a concept that is similar to Protestant ideas about the "covenant theory". This author is evidently correct in saying that Orthodox Canon Law cannot be understood except by comparative studies. Yet this should not lead one to think that there is little or nothing left of the ancient common Orthodox Canon Law. While it may be true that until now each church has endeavored to compose her own Code without much regard for the discipline of the sister churches, nonetheless, there is far more canonical unity among the Orthodox than is commonly believed. For all of them it is still true that the Code promulgated at the Council of Trullo is valid, however inapplicable. Indeed, each new Code of the individual churches officially intends to be nothing more than a modern application of the ancient canons.

Alivisatos shares the much more prevalent view that strongly champions the possibility and necessity of a unique Code for Orthodoxy. This outstanding Greek canonist has been advocating such a Code since at least 1930. In that year, a commission, preparatory to the Pan-Orthodox Synod which was to have met (but never did so) on Mount Athos in the Monastery of Vatopedi, approved a proposal of the delegates of the patriarch of Alexandria to submit to the synod the project of a Common Code for the Orthodox Churches. A few months later in the same year, Alivisatos, in a paper read at the Third Meeting of Byzantinists

[8] B. Archondonis, *Peri ten kodipoiesin tou dikaiou tes Orthodoksou Ekklesias,* an unpublished dissertation defended at the Pontifical Oriental Institute in Rome in December 1968.

[9] A. Christophilopoulos, *Hellenikon Ekklesiastikon Dikaion* (Athens, 1965), pp. 12-17.

in Belgrade, proposed the establishment of a commission in which scholars of all Orthodox churches would be represented. This commission was to prepare a code to be submitted for approval to a Pan-Orthodox Synod. The paper of Alivisatos was published next year in a book issued to honor the archbishop of Athens, Chrysostomos Papadopoulos.[10] However, nothing came of his project.

Steps toward a New Code

At the first meeting of the First Congress of Orthodox Theologians in Athens in 1936, Prof, Alivisatos, together with Prof. Sesan, proposed again and obtained the following recommendation of the Congress: "The First Congress of Orthodox Theologians, recognizing the necessity of a codification of the holy canons, expresses to the Most Holy Orthodox Churches the desire that they constitute, by common understanding and by the mediation of the patriarch of Constantinople, a commission of professors of Canon Law from the theological faculties, with the task of preparing this Code, which, once composed, shall be submitted to their approval." [11]

Once again, however, no commission was established. Nonetheless, Alivisatos continued his insistence on the necessity of a new Code for Orthodoxy.[12] In 1960, the metropolitan of Myra, Chrysostomos Constantinidis, in a fine article on *Matters That Unify and Diversify the One Orthodoxy*, upheld the same necessity.[12a] Since Metropolitan Constantinidis is the secretary of the

[10] A. Alivisatos, "He kodikopoiesis ton. Hieron kanonen tes Orthodoxou Ekklesias," in *Enaisima epi te triakoste pempte epeteridi tes epistemonikes draseos tou Makariotatou Chrysostemou Papadopoulou Archiepiskopou Athenon kai pases Hellados* (Athens, 1931), pp. 24-27.

[11] Cf. *Procés-Verbaux du premier congrès de théologie Orthodoxe à Athènes* (Athens, 1939), p. 464. For the papers of Alivisatos and Sesan read at the meeting, cf. pp. 308-23.

[12] Cf. his "He kodikopoiesis ton hieron kanonen 'ton Anatolikon Ekklesion' tes Romaiokatholikes Ekklesias," in *Theologia* 29 (1958), pp. 475-96; "He kodikopoiesis ton hieron kanonen," in *Orthodoxos Skepsis* 3 (1960), pp. 37-39.

[12a] "Semeia enounta kai diaforopoiounda ten mian Orthodoxian 'hymon'," in *Gregorios ho Palamas* 42 (1959), pp. 457-79.

Holy Synod of the Ecumenical Patriarchate, this article makes it clear that Constantinople finally intends serious actions toward a new Code. In actual fact, in the Project for the Pan-Orthodox Conference at Rhodes in 1961 there was a section on "Church Administration and Ecclesiastical Discipline" [13] which contained an almost complete outline for a Code. The Project was proposed by the Secretariat of the Holy Synod of the Ecumenical Patriarchate. This section was approved, with but slight changes, at the conference and figures now in the program for the future Pre-Synod of the Orthodox Churches. The section runs as follows:

III. CHURCH ADMINISTRATION AND ECCLESIASTICAL DISCIPLINE

A. Codification of the Holy Canons and other canonical prescriptions with a view to their eventual ratification by an ecumenical council, when the time shall have come for one.

B. Administration of Justice and Penal Procedure:
   (a) An organization of ecclesiastical courts in the entire Orthodox Church that will be as uniform as possible.
   (b) The establishment of a penal procedure that will be identical as far as possible.
   (c) Appeals.

C. Concerning Bishops:
   (a) A study of the manner of electing bishops so that it may conform to the canons as closely as possible.
   (b) Administrative and other distinctions among the bishops: (1) patriarchs; (2) heads of the autocephalous churches; (3) metropolitans; (4) archbishops; (5) titular metropolitans; (6) residential bishops; (7) titular and auxiliary bishops; (8) chorbishops.

D. Monastic Life: a search for suitable means for bringing Orthodox monastic life back to its ancient splendor by fidelity to its traditions and monastic rules and by a resumption of its former activity.

E. Adaptation of canonical prescriptions regarding fasting so as to be in accord with the exigencies of our times.

F. Formation of the Clergy:
   (a) Manner, aim and content of clerical formation.

[13] Cf. *Proche-Orient Chrétien* 9 (1961), pp. 261-66.

(b) The immediate supervision of clerical formation by the hierarchy.

(c) The formation of the clergy in theology and other fields.

(d) Lectures for the formation of clergy.

G. Marriage Impediments: a study of the actual practice of local churches and the Church's power in this field, with a view to arriving at a uniform practice in the entire Orthodox Church, as far as this is possible.

H. Deportment of Clerics: their appearance and dress.

I. The Problem of the Calendar: a study of the question based on the decision of the First Ecumenical Council in regard to the date of Easter, aiming at the establishment of a practice common to all Orthodox Churches in this matter.[14]

The approval of the above Program at Rhodes necessitated the establishment of officially recognized group of scholars, furnished with all the necessary scientific and material means, which could in a few years' time arrive at practical proposals for a Code. Until now, little has been accomplished in this direction. However, the Academy of Athens, in collaboration with the professors of the universities of Athens and Thessaloniki, announced to the press on March 5, 1965 its decision to establish a commission for a new Orthodox Code. The decision was welcomed by the ecumenical patriarch and the Holy Synod of the Greek Church. In September 1966, by a government decree, a special commission for this purpose was established with a chairman and five members. It was called the Office for the Collection and Systematization of the Holy Canons. The work of this office was supposed to be completed within six years. Already three years have passed, and there are no longer any predictions as to when the task will be finished.

Decisions of the Inter-Orthodox Commission

On June 8-15, 1968, an Inter-Orthodox Commission met at Chambesy near Geneva for the purpose of revising the proce-

---

[14] The Program is briefly but clearly explained by P. Duprey in "Les résultats de la conférence interorthodoxe de Rhodes. Le programme du futur prosynode," in *Proche-Orient Chrétien* 9 (1961), pp. 351-78.

dure adopted at Rhodes in 1961 for the preparation of the Pan-Orthodox Synod. At Rhodes it had been agreed that each single autocephalous church would study all the points of the Program (there were many more than those contained in the "third section" given above). Once this had been done, a Pro-Synod was to be convoked, which, having compared the results reached by each single church, was to draw up a preliminary document that would prepare the way for the convocation of the hoped-for Pan-Orthodox Synod. Ideal as it was in theory, the procedure was impracticable. The chief reason was that the task exceeded the capacity of most of the autocephalous churches. Furthermore, much energy and time had to be devoted to two other Rhodes Conferences in 1963 and 1964 and to the meeting of two theological commissions in Belgrade in 1967, which dealt with matters other than the Code. The Chambesy Conference of June 1968 (25 members, the majority being bishops) had for its principal task the responsibility for finding a new procedure that would lead to a quick *aggiornamento* of Orthodoxy and its approval in the Holy and Great Council of the Holy Orthodox Church of the East.

Among the many decisions of this conference,[15] the most important one seems to be the establishment of a permanent Inter-Orthodox Preparatory Commission (twelve Churches: Constantinople, Alexandria, Antioch, Jerusalem, Russia, Serbia, Rumania, Bulgaria, Cyrus, Greece, Poland, and Finland) in which each church has a member, and the creation of a permanent center in Geneva, under the responsibility of the ecumenical patriarch, to coordinate the work toward the Pan-Orthodox Synod. Moreover, to each church a portion of the Program of 1961 has been entrusted for careful study. A report on this portion in Greek and Russian should be presented within ten months to the office in Geneva, which will then communicate the reports received to all churches for their comments; these comments are to be submitted to Geneva within six months, and so on. It is

[15] There is a good commentary on this subject in *Proche-Orient Chrétien* 18 (1968), pp. 167-84.

much to be hoped that this time the deadlines will be met and that the whole procedure will reach a successful conclusion. However, the new Common Code cannot be produced in a short time. In fact, last year's Inter-Orthodox Conference has limited the study called for by the Program of 1961 to six points, putting aside for the present the "Codification of the Holy Canons and the Canonical Prescriptions" which appeared in the third section of the Program under letter A. The conference obviously considered that the practical resources of the Orthodox Churches are not yet sufficient to allow them to go ahead with a complete Code. However, if the six points are successfully investigated within the desired time limit, the way for a new Code will be opened up. The six points are the following:

1. The sources of divine revelation.

2. A greater participation of laymen in the cultural life of the Church and in other domains.

3. An adaptation of the rules on fasting (Lent), according to the exigencies of the present day.

4. Marriage impediments.

5. The problems of the calendar.

6. "Economy" and "strictness" in the Orthodox Church.

Obviously these six points would have the greatest impact on a future Code, and some of them (especially 3 and 4) would already represent the first parts of it and be valid for all Orthodox churches. The study of the first point is confided to the Church of Constantinople, the Bulgarian Church is responsible for the second on laymen, the study on fasting has been given to the Serbian Church, the Russian and the Greek Churches are entrusted with the marriage impediments and the calendar, while the Rumanian Church has the very difficult task of defining rules on *economy* or *strictness*—that is, principles for the interpretation of the Holy Canons.

Some writers appear to have the impression that the Orthodox have done no serious research toward a new Code. This impression, however, is based on an ignorance of the real state of affairs. In actual fact, at least some churches (the Greek, Serbian,

Rumanian, and also the the Russian before the Revolution)
have produced a large number of valuable canonical studies and
even Codes that are virtually the equal, as regards technique and
practicability, of the two Codes that the Catholic Church has
produced in this century for the Latin and Oriental Catholic
Churches.

The Russian Church, in 1917-1918 in its Pan-Russian Synod,
enacted a Code on patriarchs, diocesan administration, parishes,
monks and some other matters, which was the result of fifteen
years of research, studies, discussions and debates that followed
fifty years of development in canonical science under the guidance of such professors as Pavlov, Beneševič, Berdnikov,
Suvorov, Gorčakov and others.[16]

A great deal of canonical work has also been accomplished
during the last forty years in the Serbian Church, which has what
is perhaps the best and most homogeneus code on the
patriarch, synod, bishops, marriage, ecclesiastical punishments,
etc.[17]

In Rumania canonical studies are florishing, as is proved by
numerous profound articles in some excellent theological journals,
the "Statutes" promulgated by this church in 1948, and twelve
"Regulations" issued in the years following. Stan has written two
recent articles explaining the development of Canon Law in
Rumania and setting down the fundamental principles of Orthodox Canon Law which should guide the composers of the new
Code.[18] According to him, an Orthodox Code should be based on

[16] Concerning this synod, cf. N. Zernov, *The Russian Religious Renaissance of the Twentieth Century* (London, 1963), and "The Reform
of the Church and the Pre-Revolutionary Russian Episcopate," in *St.
Vladimir's Seminary Quarterly* 6 (1962), pp. 128-38; M. Benigsen, "The
Year 1917 in the History of the Russian Church," *ibid.* 7 (1963), pp.
115-32; A. Wuyts, *Le patriarcat russe au Concile de Moscou de 1917-
1918* (Rome, 1941); I. Rezac, *De Monachismo secundum recentiorem
legislationem russicam* (Rome, 1952); M. Prichodjko, *Die Pfarrei in
der neueren Gesetzgebung der Russischen Kirche* (Brixen, 1947).

[17] The best treatment of this subject is the book of V. Pospischil, *Der
Patriarch in der Serbisch Orthodoxen Kirche* (Vienna, 1966); cf. its review in *Orientalia Christiana Periodica* 32 (1966), pp. 573-75.

[18] L. Stan, "La législation de l'Eglise Orthodoxe de Roumanie pen-

eight principles closely connected with dogma and on four others of a purely "canonical" nature. These are: (1) the divine-human nature of the (2) universal Church in which every member (3) collaborates in the work for the salvation of souls, under the guidance of (4) a hierarchy organized in (5) a synodal system. The exercise of ecclesiastical authority should be governed by the principles of (6) *economy,* (7) an independence of, and, at the same time, (8) loyalty to the civil power, (9) the autocephalous character of the churches, (10) an autonomy with regard to a superior Orthodox authority, (11) the acceptance of State laws in the ecclesiastical Codes or the "nomocanonical principle", and, finally, (12) the territorial principle, according to which boundaries of dioceses and parishes should correspond to the administrative divisions of the State.

There is no need to mention here again the merits of the Greek canonists of this century of the universities of Athens and Thessaloniki, men like Alivisatos, Cotsonis (now the archbishop of Athens and all Greece), Mouratides, Christophilopoulos and several others. Suffice it to say that, in view of the Codes that have already been revamped in some churches and of the valuable works published in recent years by Orthodox canonists, pessimism with regard to the task of preparing for a Common Code does not seem to be justified.

---

dant le patriarcat de sa Beatitude le Patriarche Justinien," in *Ortodoxia* 20 (1968), pp. 276-96 (in Rumanian), and "Peri ton themeliodon kanonikon archon tes Orthodoxias," in *Theologia* 39 (1968), pp. 7-18.

PART III
DOCUMENTATION
CONCILIUM

Office of the Executive Secretary
Nijmegen, Netherlands

Concilium General Secretariat/*Nijmegen, Netherlands*

Human Rights

To forestall misunderstanding about an article [1] on human rights in this Canon Law volume, it has to be pointed out beforehand that the word "right" in the phrase "human rights" does not have the same strict meaning which it has in the discipline of Canon Law. The Declaration of Human Rights, solemnly proclaimed by the United Nations in Paris on December 10, 1948, is the ideal formulation of the position which every human being should be entitled to in any juridical system. As such the rights formulated in Paris cannot be enforced, but they express the ideal position of every human being in a juridical situation based on the dignity of the human person. They express not so much what has been achieved in matters of justice by an advancing culture, as an end to attain. They call for the

[1] This article is the result of the efforts of a study group which consisted of the team of the General Secretariate and the cooperation of J. Donders, P. Huizing and J. Rietmeijer. An article concerning Church law needs the work of the *Centre de Recherche et de Documentation des Institutions Chrétiennes,* set up by René Metz and Jean Schlick at the University of Strasbourg (CERDIC); it has started in September 1969 to publish an annual bibliography about ecclesiastical institutions, with key words in five languages. For this, as for the evaluation of articles, it makes use of a computer system, and will include Anglican, Orthodox and Protestant publications. The Center also organizes a conference every year on the most urgent juridical issues. The topic for May 1970 will be the bond of marriage. The address is: CERDIC, Place de l'Université 67, Strasbourg, France.

progressive realization of the ideal formulated in the Declaration for all human beings in every juridical system and all legislation. The Declaration is a living and dynamic statement which has contributed much in twenty years to the maintenance and protection of the inalienable rights of man and his fundamental freedoms.

This inspiring influence of the Declaration has been reinforced by agreements between groups of countries to bind themselves to a more strict observation of these human rights. Thus there are already several agreements in existence, such as the European Agreement between sixteen States, where the human rights mentioned are bolstered by an international machinery which guarantees the observation of the obligations these States have accepted—for instance, the Court of Europe at Strasbourg. All members of the Council of Europe, apart from France and Switzerland, have accepted this European Agreement as binding. This framework also provides a juridical procedure valid for both the particular States and individual persons, though only in the case of those States that have accepted it explicitly.

In this way the Declaration has indirectly exercised a great influence on the legislation of particular States, although there is in general some hesitation about embodying the Declaration in their constitutions. This again points to the peculiar character of these rights: they are postulates that precede legislation but can no longer be ignored or limited by this legislation. In this sense the Declaration can also exercise its influence on the juridical order within the Churches and the codification of a new Canon Law. Thus in this article we shall seek (1) to remember the historical development of these human rights, since they constitute a provisional term to what Christian culture has achieved; (2) to see what kind of response the Declaration has found to date in the Catholic and other Christian Churches; (3) to look for possible improvements in the present juridical system in the Catholic Church on the basis of this Declaration. With this in mind one might point to some indications that are relevant for the juridical system of the Church in the future.

I

THE HISTORICAL GROWTH OF THE DECLARATION [2]

The general purport of the Declaration is that all men have inalienable rights and are fundamentally equal in dignity by the pure and simple fact of their being human. This fundamental equality of all human beings is one of the key points of the Christian message and perhaps the most revolutionary element in the Gospel. If this fundamental equality has been interpreted by the Christian tradition as "an equality before God", this addition may in practice mean a limitation of human rights. But at the same time this implies the recognition of the equality of all men among themselves, even though in practice this recognition has always been accompanied by revolution. Here one thinks of Camus' words: "The spirit of revolution can only exist in a society where an equality in theory hides gross inequalities in fact."

Wherever in history one talks about progress in the formulation of the rights of man, there has always been protest and the breakthrough of a vision of deliverance, however limited, in preparation for it. History also shows that the universal extension of these rights proceeds in quantity and quality, starting with

[2] For the origins of the Declaration, cf. P. de la Chapelle, *La déclaration universelle des Droits de l'homme et le Catholicisme* (Paris, 1967), pp. viii and 490 (somewhat apologetic in character); Commission on Human Rights, *Report on the 21st Session: Jan. 29—Feb. 19, 1968* (New York, 1968), *Yearbook of the United Nations* (1946ff.); R. MacIver, *Great Expressions of Human Rights* (New York, 1950); G. Oestreich, *Die Idee der Menschenrechte in ihrer geschichtlichen Entwicklung* (Wolfenbüttel, 1961); J. Roche, *All Men Are Created Equal* (The Franklin Memorial Lectures, Detroit, 1966); P. Modinos, *Introduction à l'étude des droits de l'homme* (Strasbourg, 1963); L. Rubio Garcia, *Hacia un nuevo orden internacional* (Madrid, 1968). For specialized organizations and particular agreements, see the list in *Bulletin of the International Commission of Jurists* 32 (Dec. 1967), p. 8; *Human Rights and the United Nations Family* (New York, 1968). N. Luhmann, in *Grundrechte als Institution* (Berlin, 1965), points out that as the rights of man extend in our society and take deeper root in the social order, society becomes more pluriform, yet can become more integrated in spite of the growing diversity.

the Magna Carta (June 15, 1215) which is popularly seen as a beginning of the formulation of human rights. In fact, it bestowed privileges on the feudal nobility and ecclesiastical authorities over against the king, but the group endowed with these rights constituted only a small section compared with the mass of those left without rights. When the people no longer recognized their own voice in that of the Church, they formulated their own rights in the English Bill of Rights (1689).

Scholastic teaching about natural law as a participation in the eternal law of God, Spanish Scholasticism, particularly that of de Vitoria, and Hugo de Groot's great work on the law of nations all provided a theoretical basis for human rights, but the further development of this was blocked in Europe by the increase in religious intolerance, which contrasted sharply with the theory of humanism and rather played into the hands of the absolute monarchy. The Enlightenment created a favorable climate for the rights and liberties of the individual over against society. In the New World the colonials made themselves free of the European homeland (the American Declaration of Independence of July 4, 1776 and the American Bill of Rights of 1789), but the quantitative extension of human rights was not yet sufficiently advanced to apply these rights of man to the colonized people themselves. On this point the South American States were more advanced in their legislation than those of North America. The rights of man, as formulated in the Declaration of Independence and the Constitution of the United States, only applied to those who were thought of as "men" by their fellow citizens—that is, as "American" men. At first, this excluded Negroes, Catholics and atheists.

The ideas of Milton, Hobbes and Locke led the development of the rights of man to Rousseau's *Contrat Social*, which became a political reality in the French Revolution: man has his own original value, independent of the State. His rights and liberties, laid down in the *Déclaration des Droits de l'homme et du Citoyen*, are inalienable: freedom, property, security, resistance to oppression. In actual fact, however, these rights became the privileges of a successful and confident *bourgeoisie*. The French *Déclaration* of 1789 was followed by the Communist Manifesto and the Russian Revolution of October 1917. In his speech on the four freedoms [3] of January 6, 1941, Roosevelt tried to make human rights universal both in extension and in quality. The fact that somebody is a human person entitles him to these freedoms. This holds for everyone from birth, and his rights are related to the whole of man's existence. That this does not yet exhaust all the implications of a true universality in this matter of human rights is proved by, among other factors, the student revolutions, [4] where particularly the younger generation claims other, sometimes very radical, applications of this universality. The rights of man are therefore not something static but constitute a dynamic reality which will continue to operate in a way that may be unexpected or even undesired.

What has been formulated so far, however, is a number of postulates which can no longer be ignored by national legislation or by the statutory law of particular religious societies. [5] The rights of man express the fundamental dignity of man. The prac-

[3] These four freedoms are of two kinds: freedom *of* and freedom *from*—freedom *of* speech and expression, freedom *of* every person to worship God in his own way, freedom *from* want and freedom *from* fear.

[4] Cf. "Revolution in the Universities: The Moral Problem," in *Concilium* 45 (1969). There often is a danger that the demand for all rights for everybody will become a new myth; cf. "La droit à la santé—mythe ou réalité," in a special issue of *Cahiers Laennec* (March, 1967).

[5] "Dossier sur les droits de l'homme," in *Doc. Cath.* (1949), pp. 401-28 and 478-90; *ibid.* (Nov. 1968), p. 1999; special issue of *Lumen Vitae* 23 (1968), pp. 593-674; J. Maritain, *Les droits de l'homme et la loi naturelle* (New York, 1943); L. de Naurois, "Introduction à l'étude des droits et libertés de l'homme," in *Rev. de Droit Can.* 14 (1964), pp. 221-40; C. van Boven, *Rechten van de mens op nieuwe paden* (Deventer, 1968); R. Gardiner, "Christianity and Human Rights," in *The Ecumenical Review* 20 (Oct. 1968), pp. 404-09; O. Nolde, "Human Rights in Retrospect—A Contemporary Appraisal," *ibid.,* pp. 395-403; M. Rowe, "Cloistered Human Rights," in *New Christian* 83 (Nov. 1968), p. 6; A. Messineo, "La promozione dei diritti dell'uomo," in *Civ. Catt.* 119 (Dec. 1968), pp. 478-82; "Bene commune e diritti del'uomo alla 39-a Settimana sociale dei Cattolici Italiani," *ibid.* (Oct. 1968), pp. 105-09. Two Catholic organizations deserve special mention for their influence on the drafting of the Declaration: the World Organization of Catholic

tical recognition and promotion of this dignity precedes the acceptance of the Declaration. This has not been realized by all in the States that have signed the Declaration. The constitutions of communist countries, for instance, indeed mention these rights to freedom, including freedom of speech, freedom of the press and freedom of association, but in practice the underlying anthropology often turns them into a caricature. It would therefore be utopian to think that a new formulation of Canon Law would only gain by embodying this Declaration in a new Code.

Now that the rights of man have been formulated, the Declaration is criticized for being too humanistic (Arab countries), too Western (communist and developing countries), too individualistic (both the Soviet block and the Arab countries abstained when the definitive Declaration was put to a vote), or too little religious (the Christian Churches). Insofar as this last point is concerned, it is often overlooked that, in historical fact, the United States Constitution (together with its jurisprudence) is the only one to be derived from a Christian tradition, while Canon Law owes very much to Hellenistic and Roman influences.

II
REPERCUSSIONS TO THE DECLARATION WITHIN THE CHRISTIAN CHURCHES

In the Catholic Church

It is an acknowledged fact that, apart from the positive influence of South American legislation, the North American hierarchy supported the "four freedoms" of Roosevelt before the Declaration was signed. During the debates of Vatican II, particularly in connection with the conciliar *Declaration on Religious Freedom,* one could sense the concern with the rights of man, particularly

Women, represented by C. Schaeffer and M. de Romer, and the International Confederation of Christian Trade Unions, represented by A. Vanistendael.

when the North American hierarchy intervened. They were supported in this by the unequivocal statements about human rights in the encyclical *Pacem in terris* which, after the anti-modernist *Quanta cura, Mirari vos* and the famous Syllabus of Errors, passed from the timid and hesitant admission of human rights by Leo XIII to a definite and convincing conclusion. The basic elements for this encyclical of John XXIII were derived from addresses given by Pius XII, particularly that of December 24, 1942 (*AAS* 35 [1943], pp. 9-24). The fact that the U.N. Declaration left out any religious argument on principle raised some eyebrows in ecclesiastical circles, where this was seen as a legacy from the Enlightenment and Modernism. The official message of Paul VI to the Conference of Teheran on the occasion of the 20th anniversary of the Declaration opens with a reference to these objections and points to the visible gap between theory and practice where the rights of man are concerned. He criticized the third point of the Declaration, the right to resist any oppression, but he saw positive good in the fact that the Declaration can contribute to the organization of the world community. Although he makes use of phrases employed by John XXIII, one senses in Pope Paul a certain reserve. Apparently he would like to have human rights more explicitly based on natural law and God and to use them as a guarantee for the arrival of the kingdom of God.[6]

In general the reaction of Rome has been positive and favorable. When we compare this attitude with, for instance, that of the Catholic authorities to the French *Déclaration,* we see that there has been a definite development. If the opening of the *Declaration of Religious Freedom* of Vatican II clearly shows

[6] "Message du Pape Paul VI à la Conférence de Téhéran," in *Doc. Cath.* 1517 (May 19, 1968), pp. 881-84. *Sacramentum Mundi* III (Freiburg, 1969) contains an interesting survey by J. Diez Alegría linking the Declaration with the encyclicals, particularly those of Leo XIII and Pius XII. This also shows how a long and laborious dialectic between ecclesiastical thought and the ideas of the Enlightenment and the French Revolution has led to a positive synthesis which is reflected in several documents of Vatican II (on the missions, religious freedom, non-Christian religions, and the Church in the modern world).

some reservations where it is a matter of putting this religious freedom into practice by Rome itself (since it is principally concerned with religious oppression by the State), in practice the new Secretariates for Christian Unity and for Non-Believers show a more loyal application of this freedom on the part of the Church.

The Other Christian Churches

Apart from the fact that the Anglican Churches considered the Declaration as wholly obvious and the Orthodox totally ignored it, one may say that the Protestant Churches reacted both very critically and yet positively. The formulation of the rights originated in a religious culture which had been humanized, particularly in Anglo-Saxon countries. But when it came to thinking about the ideas that lay behind the Declaration, Protestant theologians in particular were rather worried about the unmentioned a-Christian foundation which they thought they could spy behind these rights and about the reemergence of a kind of natural law in disguise. These Christian Churches often criticize the fact that these rights seem to be based on a humanistic belief (opening of the Declaration) which appears to exclude revelation.[7]

In the World Council of Churches, interest is no longer as keen as it was.[8] Since the Geneva Conference of 1966 about the place of the Church in society, an increasing number of member

[7] The Orthodox delegate for Lebanon, C. Habib Malik, constantly insisted at the drafting of the Declaration on a wording which was consonant with the Christian concept of human dignity; A. Verdoodt, *Naissance et signification de la Déclaration universelle des droits de l'homme* (Louvain, 1964).

[8] "Message from the President of the World Council of Churches for Human Rights Day," in *The Ecumenical Review* 21 (April 1969), pp. 167-68; U. Scheuner, "Zum Jahr der Menschenrechte," in *Luther. Monatsh.* 7 (1968), pp. 616-19; J. de Graaf, "Theologische achtergronden van het manifest van de Rechten van de mens," in *Rondom het Woord* 11 (Feb. 1969), pp. 47-57; A. Rasker, "De universele Verklaring aangaande de rechten van de mens—axioma of experiment?" in *De Rechten van de Mens* (Leiden, 1968); O. Nolde, *Free and Equal* (Geneva, 1968); W. Dantine, "Verantwortung für das Recht als Forderung des Glaubens," in *Evangelische Theologie* 29 (Jan. 1969), pp. 24-40.

Churches, particularly in developing countries, want to give priority to problems that look more pressing than the Declaration. After all, only a thin upper layer of the world's population, the limited group of those who enjoy economic prosperity, can more or less take advantage of these rights. As R. Shaull, among others, put it, in the eyes of the younger Christian Churches in developing countries, what previous revolutions have achieved in terms of freedom has long ago become the new establishment. Since July 1966 ecumenical thought about social morality has changed from "an ethic of order to an ethic of change" (Lochman), and there is an explicit demand for a theology of revolution (Lehmann). Yet, from Amsterdam to Uppsala the World Council has been concerned about the rights of man. Their theological train of thought might be summarized as follows: The Declaration of the Rights of Man is, anthropologically speaking, a minimum; it is not good enough for theology to justify this minimum theologically; on the contrary, this minimum should be taken as a challenge to theology itself to give more thought to the relationship between God, man and society. The moralizing warning that the Church should always remember that she has been the teacher, from almost every point of view, of the totalitarian State is really too one-sided (Brunner). In Scripture man is a much more problematic creature than the optimistic Declaration of the Rights of Man would lead us to believe. This holds also for the freedom to which the Gospel summons us and the freedom of the Declaration.

While it seems impossible to achieve unanimity on the basic reasons for these rights of man,[9] or, rather, while there are various

[9] The contributions, particularly of C. Perelman, N. Bobbio, L. Russel, A. van Melsen and J. Hyppolite, to *Le fondement des Droits de l'Homme—Actes et entretiens de l'Aquila, 14-19 Sept., 1964* (Florence, 1966) show how much opinions can differ about the basic arguments for the rights of man. A previous inquiry among the participants in this event revealed that nobody wanted to found these rights in a natural or a transcendental order, while everybody agreed that to vindicate them on historical grounds alone was not satisfactory either. In Russia basic social rights are more heavily emphasized than freedom rights; see R. Cassin, "Twenty Years after the Universal Declaration," in *Journal of the International Commission of Jurists* (Dec. 1967), pp. 6-7.

ways by which one can come to recognize these rights, the most important factor is that they must be recognized in practice.

III
HUMAN RIGHTS AND CHURCH ORDER

The determination to create a juridical order which safeguards the personal freedom of man should also be expressed in Church order. One would even expect the Church to set an example here: Church law ought to be a living theological expression of man's rights by its very nature.[10] I want to illustrate this by giving some examples of how human rights can be embodied in Church order.

The Specific Nature of Church Order

The specific character of legal relationships within the ecclesial community lies in that the faithful not only have their own autonomous freedom with regard to each other, but are all personally united to the Lord and are all personally responsible to him. The factors which constitute this community are the deeds performed by the community in the name and person of the Lord: the sacraments. The key function of a Church order as well as its aim is to protect and guarantee this proper responsibility in faith and its development. The quality of the ecclesial community as a sacramental community of faith is decisive for the nature and function of Church law.

Particular Rights

1. *Equality and Brotherhood*.[11] The first Article of the Declaration says: "All human beings are born free and equal in dignity and rights. They are endowed with reason and conscience and should act toward one another in a spirit of brotherhood."

[10] A. Rouco Varela, "Was ist 'Katholische Rechtstheologie'?" in *Archiv für kath. Kirchenrecht* 135 (1966), pp. 530-43.
[11] I have borrowed the headings from P. de la Chapelle, *op. cit.*

At Vatican II the need was felt to give fresh expression to the evangelical principle of the fundamental equality of all the faithful.[12] Civil society today does not tolerate a situation in which certain people have rights which express personal superiority over others. A "personality cult" is not recognized in law. On this point Church order is not exactly an example. Recent timid attempts to reduce claims to superiority symbols barely effect the backwardness of the Church in this field.[13] Church law should radically and resolutely reject any claims that might suggest inequality among the faithful on principle, whatever the function. Claims to symbols with a liturgical meaning cannot be extended and degraded to claims to symbols of personal reverence let alone glorification.

2. *No Discrimination.* Article 2 of the Declaration rejects any form of discrimination.[14] Here the impression created by our Church order is far more favorable. In law the issue of race or color is totally irrelevant. Since Pius XI the formation of an indigenous clergy and hierarchy has been actively pursued. This can rightly be called an exemplary encouragement of the younger nations in their striving for political autonomy. In law, birth and

[12] *Constitution on the Church,* n. 32.

[13] The Latin text of *Ut sive sollicite* appeared in *L'Osserv. Rom.* (April 6, 1969); cf. *Doc. Cath.* 51 (April 20, 1969), cc. 364-66.

[14] *Towards a Declaration of Christian Freedoms,* a symposion on a Declaration of Christian Freedoms sponsored by the Canon Law Society of America and the Catholic University of America, Washington D.C., held October 5-6, 1968: "All members of the Church are entitled to all rights and freedoms of Christians without discrimination on the basis of race, color, sex, birth, language, political opinion, national or social origin"; I. Beyer, "De iuribus humanis fundamentalibus in statuto iuridico christifidelium assumendis," in *Periodica* 58 (1969), pp. 29-58; J. Delanglade, "Nécessité et urgence de la réforme du droit canon," in *Etudes* (June 1969), pp. 894-905. It is interesting to notice that the Commission for the Declaration of Human Rights ran into difficulties when it wanted to declare that legitimate and illegitimate children had equal rights in law. The proposal to give illegitimate chidren the same *rights* as the legitimate ones, though supported by Soviet countries, Scandinavian countries and South America, was defeated. The Commission had to be satisfied with: "All children, whether born in or out of wedlock, shall enjoy the same social protection" (Art. 25, 2); cf. V. Saario, *Study of Discrimination Against Persons Born out of Wedlock* (New York, 1967), pp. 16-20 and 191-93.

social background have no claims to special privileges. In fact, no notice is taken of this in matters of appointments to ecclesiastical functions and offices. Insofar as language and nationality are concerned, the law is replacing the factual preponderence of Italians in curial positions by more international appointments.[15] Ecclesiastical discrimination on grounds of political opinion has recently been declared illegal by the recognition of any autonomy in politics.[16]

Where discrimination on the basis of sex is concerned, the situation is less healthy. The position of women in Church order, particularly of female religious,[17] is still plainly one of discrimination. It is urgently necessary for the law to radically abolish the still legally existing "minority status" of secular and regular female superiors, even in matters of going out and dress, and to give them a position equal to that of their male colleagues.

3. *Equality in the Administration of Justice*.[18] Canon Law recognizes the principle that anybody can seek protection for any right he has within the community by taking his case to an ecclesiastical tribunal (C. 1667). The fourth book of the Code gives details about the jurisdiction involved and the legal procedure. This right to action is drastically limited by the fact that one cannot take complaints about administrative decisions taken by ordinaries to court. In theory there is controversy about the point whether this kind of complaint is not admitted because of supposed injustice in administration or because a right has been infringed. In practice, the latter case never occurs. One can only lodge a complaint against a decision taken by an authority by taking it to a higher authority—namely, one of the Roman

---

[15] Apost. Const. *Regimini Ecclesiae Universae* in *Doc. Cath.* 49 (Sept. 3, 1967), cc. 1442-73; *Decree on the Pastoral Office of Bishops in the Church*, n. 10: ". . . optantur ut eorum membra, officiales et consultores necnon legati Romani Pontificis . . . ex diversis Ecclesiae regionibus assumantur. . . ."

[16] *Decree on the Apostolate of the Laity*, nn. 7, 13-14.

[17] M. Rowe, *art. cit.*; V. Walsh, "Pacem in Terris: The Religious Sister and the Revision of Canon Law," in *The Jurist* (1966), pp. 460-64.

[18] *Declaration of Christian Freedoms*, n. 10: "All members of the Church have a right to effective remedies for the redress of grievances and the vindication of their rights."

Congregations. And against the decision by such a Congregation one can only ask for a retrial of the case by the same Congregation. Since the reform of the curia it has become possible to appeal against a decision by an organ of the curia by going to the Apostolic Signature, if it is felt that the decision has infringed one's rights.[19] The result of all this is that ecclesiastical tribunals only deal with marital cases, while genuine processes about valid legal cases are extremely rare.

To this must be added that in practice if not in theory justice is administered as if it were a favor granted by the authority, is dispensed without involving the interested parties, and very often ends with the communication of a decision without giving the reasons for that decision. This obscures the whole matter of justice. In a sacramental community of faith it is extremely important that the legal way of protecting one's ecclesial rights is clear, public and open to every member with regard to every other member, whosoever it may be, and every level of authority. The principle that "the first See cannot be judged by anyone" (C. 1556) also ought to be qualified, as is already proved by the institution of the Apostolic Signature as judge in cases involving departments of the curia.[20]

4. *Impartial Justice.* The existence and effective functioning of independent and impartial justice[21] is a service to both parties and prevents many conflicts that are otherwise insoluble. When, for instance, there is a conflict between a bishop and one of his clergy and this priest thinks his rights have been infringed, it is practically impossible for the bishop himself or some other authority dependent on him to solve it. A solution which will also satisfy the community can only be given by an impartial judge who is not dependent on the bishop. From this point of view it is not really satisfactory in the technical sense for the Apostolic

[19] Apost. Const. *Regimini Ecclesiae universae,* n. 106; cf. *Doc. Cath.* 49 (Sept. 3, 1967), c. 1468.
[20] K. Fink, "Zum Thema: Papstabsetzung im Mittelalter," in *Theol. Quart.* 149 (1969), pp. 185-89.
[21] There is a striking similarity between Articles 9, 10 and 11 of the Declaration and the plea for theological freedom published by a group of *Concilium* theologians.

Signature—itself a cardinalitial body—to judge cases involving cardinalitial congregations. Article 11 of the Declaration should lead in Church law to the abolition of the so-called "suspension *ex informata conscientia*" (C. 2186-94). The reform of the curia has given the Congregation for Doctrine certain indications to be followed in procedures of penal law.[22]

5. *Respect for Private Life.* The right to a genuine private life, formulated in Article 12 of the Declaration, again reminds those in the Church of the religious, particularly female religious, who are not adequately protected by Church law against almost unlimtied interference in private affairs or who live in circumstances and under regulations that make even a minimum of privacy impossible.

6. *Freedom of Thought, Conscience and Religion.* At the start of this article I referred to the influence Article 18 has had on the conciliar *Decree on Religious Freedom.* The Council accepted the principle of religious freedom with regard to any coercion by authority in society, but the conciliar statement does not deal with the consequences of this principle to situations and relations within the Church. One consequence at least must be that the Church renounces any appeal to the secular arm (cf. C. 2198). Church law is meant to order the life of the sacramental community of believers and therefore presupposes a free acceptance of the faith. The very validity of Church law depends on this free acceptance. There is no sense in imposing Church law on people who do not believe themselves bound by such a law and who want to have no part in that community.

7. *Freedom of Opinion and Expression.* As formulated in Article 19 of the Declaration, this freedom also presupposes the right to information.[23] In this connection it would appear that,

---

[22] Cf. note 19, n. 36.

[23] A particularly well-balanced formulation on this subject has been made by the Canon Law Society of America. Progress has also been made with the formulation of the rights of the theologian. Stanley Stuber, for thirteen years chairman of the Commission on Religious Liberty of the Baptist World Alliance, published his *Universal Declaration of Rights for Theologians,* which however raises some difficulties since it starts not only from legal grounds but also from some specifically theological

at least at the level of central government, the usual ecclesiastical policy of presuming the necessity of secrecy and of only occasionally allowing publicity should be reversed so that the necessity of publicity is presumed and secrecy only occasionally imposed when there are compelling reasons for it.

8. *Freedom of Assembly and Association.* This principle, contained in Article 20 of the Declaration, seems to be sufficiently ensured in Church law. In general the freedom of personal decisions is guaranteed, particularly for the choice of the marital state and for a spiritual or religious life (C. 214; 542, par. 1; 552, par. 2; 572, par. 1, point 4; 973, par. 2; 1020, par. 2; 1074; 1081, par. 1; 1087; 2352; 2353). The principles which govern freedom of association in the Church have been set out in the *Constitution on the Church* and the *Decree on the Apostolate of the Laity.*[24]

9. *Democracy.* The right to take part in the government and to have equal access to public service in one's country as expressed in Article 21 is at present honored in the Church, insofar as there is no discrimination in admission to offices, with the exception of the still controverted issue of the admission of women to these offices. For the rest the only criterion for admission to office is that of suitability.

There have been authoritative demands for the development of more democratic structures in the Church.[25] Some clear signs of

---

opinions. In Spain both conservative and progressive theologians have published declarations as a result of the statement published by the *Concilium* theologians in December 1968: M. Alcala, "Declarationes de téologos," in *Razon y Fe* 854 (March 1969), pp. 246-52. Some restraint in bringing out new declarations might be advisable if we do not want to achieve the opposite of what was aimed at in the beginning; cfr. *idem,* "La Iglesia y la información," *loc. cit.* 852 (Jan. 1969), pp. 14-17; "Freiheit des Denkens im kirchlichen Raum," in *Wort und Wahrheit* 24 (May-June 1969), pp. 195-205.

[24] *Constitution on the Church,* n. 37; *Decree on the Apostolate of the Laity,* ch. 5; O. ter Reegen, "The Rights of the Laity," in *Concilium* 38 (1968).

[25] H. Küng, "Mitentscheidung der Laien in der Kirchenleitung und bei kirchlichen Wahlen," in *Theol. Quart.* 149 (1969), pp. 147-65. The list of questions put to Msgr. Illich blatantly contradicted this theory

this already exist in the consultation of clergy and laity for the choice of a bishop, the consultation of all members of religious societies for the revision of their constitutions,[26] and the institution of the episcopal synod,[27] councils of clergy and pastoral councils.

The tension between the necessary unity among the members and the bond of all with Christ cannot be solved by any power whatever, not even that of the democratic fifty percent plus one. The indispensable condition for the further development of democratic structures within the Church is the development of each one's awareness of his own personal responsibility to the Lord.

10. *Participation in the Cultural life of the Community.* Article 27 of the Declaration and nn. 4-5 of the Declaration on Christian Freedoms suggest the following thoughts in conclusion. If we see the Church as the sacramental community of faith, the function of the communal relationships and their regulation is to assist the growth of the life of faith in the members and in the community. This growth takes place first of all in the human persons themselves and in the groups where they confess their faith together. Central leadership will only take measures for all the Churches insofar as this is required in order to preserve the necessary unity. The Spirit of the Lord is free to inspire all Churches as he pleases. The central leadership has to follow and stimulate this inspiration, not to substitute its own initiatives for it. It is to be expected that the coordination of local developments in the one community of the world will require the central leadership to exercise a critical function with regard to this development. While maintaining their right to freedom and individuality,

---

and what has been said under section 3: J. M. D(omenach), "Illich au Saint Office," in *Esprit* 37 (May 1969), pp. 922-94; "Le questionnaire 'Illich'," in *La Revue Nouvelle* 25 (March 1969), pp. 313-24; *Nat. Cath. Reporter* 5 (Feb. 12, 1969), p. 6.

[26] Motu Proprio *Ecclesiae Sanctae* (Aug. 6, 1966); cf. *Doc. Cath.* 48 (Sept. 4, 1966), cc. 1441-70.

[27] F. Klostermann, "Supranational Episcopal Conferences," in *Concilium* 38 (1968).

the local communities should show some consideration for this delicate function of the central leadership and not always damn the restraining, or rather critical, effects of this function as conservative. No doubt, responsibility for the development of the Catholic world community lies also with every local community, but this responsibility requires dialogue and cooperation with the central leadership. In this sense the Universal Declaration of Human Rights can be an inspiration, not only for a new codification of Christian rights in a new Church order, but also for the growth of a social law, as has already happened in the legislation of many nations.

BIOGRAPHICAL NOTES

JOHANNES NEUMANN: Born in Germany in 1929, he was ordained in 1955. He studied at the universities of Freiburg-im-Breisgau and Munich, receiving a degree in theology and a doctorate in Canon Law. He is professor of Canon Law at the Faculty of Theology at the University of Tübingen. His published works include *Die Kirche und die kirchliche Gewalt vom Ende der Aufklarung bis zum Ersten Vatikanischen Konzil in der deutschen Kirchenrechtswissenschaft* (Tübingen, 1969) and *Der Spender der Firmung in der Kirche des Abendlandes* (Meitingen, 1963).

WILHELM STEINMÜLLER: Born in Germany in 1934, he is a Catholic. He studied at the University of Munich, receiving his doctorate in law in 1959. He is professor of Canon Law, of the history of Church law, and of the philosophy of law at the Faculty of Catholic Theology at Regensburg, Germany, and he contributed to *Evangelische Rechtstheologie, Zweireichelehre, Christokratie, Gnadenrecht* (Cologne-Graz, 1968).

HANS DOMBOIS: Born in Berlin in 1907, he is a Lutheran. He studied in Germany at the universities of Göttingen, Berlin and Marburg, receiving his doctorate in law in 1950. He is dean of studies for matrimonial and family law at the Faculty of Theology of Heidelberg University. His published works include *Naturrecht und christliche Existenz* (Kasser, 1952) and *Das Recht der Gnade* (Witten, 1961).

PAUL WINNINGER: Born in France in 1920, he was ordained in 1944. He studied at the University of Strasbourg, and in Paris at the Catholic Institute and the Sorbonne. He holds licentiates in theology, Canon Law, social sciences and literature, and since 1946 he has been professor of philosophy at the minor seminary of Walbourg, France. Since 1965 he has been dean of studies of religious sociology at the Faculty of Theology at Strasbourg. His published works include *Le Livre de la Famille* (Paris, 1965), and *Les Diacres. Histoire et avenir du diaconat* (Paris 1968).

JOSÉ SETIÉN: Born in Spain in 1928, he was ordained in 1951. He studied at the Gregorian in Rome, receiving his licentiate in theology and his doctorate in Canon Law (1957). Since 1957 he has been professor of ecclesiastical law at the University of Salamanca, and director

179

of the Social College for Clergy in Vitoria, Spain. His published works include *La Iglesia y lo social* (1964), and *Iglesia y libertades políticas* (1965).

PEDRO LOMBARDÍA: Born in Spain in 1930, he is a Catholic. He studied in Spain at the universities of Granada and Madrid, and in Rome at the University of St. Thomas. He holds doctorates in law and Canon Law, and since 1960 he has been professor of Canon Law at the University of Navarre in Pamplona. The editor of the review *Ius Canonicum*, he is the author of many important articles on Canon Law and its reform.

BRUNO PRIMETSHOFER, C.SS.R.: Born in Austria in 1929, he was ordained in 1954. He studied in Austria at the universities of Vienna and Innsbruck, in Rome at the Lateran, and in Germany at the University of Munich. He has been professor of Canon Law at the University of Linz since 1967. He is the author of *Ehe und Konkordat* (Vienna, 1960) and *Rechtsgeschichte der gemischten Ehen in Österreich und Ungarn 1781-1841* (Vienna, 1967).

JAN RIETMEIJER, S.J.: Born in Holland in 1917, he was ordained in 1947. He studied in Holland at the University of Nijmegen, and in Rome at the Gregorian, receiving a degree in law and a licentiate in Canon Law. He is scientific adviser on Canon Law at the Faculty of Theology at the University of Nijmegen. His writings include "De Positie van de verdachte in de kanonieke strafprocedure," in *Annalen van het Thijmgenooschap* (May, 1962).

GIOVANNI ŘEZÁČ, S.J.: Born in Czechoslovakia in 1914, he was ordained in 1943. He studied in Rome at the Gregorian and Lateran universities. With a licentiate in theology and a doctorate in *utroque Iure*, he is professor of Oriental Canon Law at the Pontifical Oriental Institute in Rome, and at the Gregorian. His published works include his thesis, *De monachismo secundum recentiorem legislationem russicam* (Rome, 1952).

ANDREW GREELEY: Born in Illinois in 1928, he was ordained in 1954. He studied at the Seminary of St. Mary of the Lake and at the University of Chicago, receiving a licentiate in theology and a doctorate in sociology. He is a lecturer in the department of sociology at the University of Chicago, where he also serves as Senior Study Director of the National Opinion Research Center. His many publications include *The Hesitant Pilgrim: American Catholicism* (New York, 1966) and *A Future To Hope In* (New York, 1969).

IVAN ŽUŽEK, S.J.: Born in Yugoslavia in 1924, he was ordained in 1955. He studied in Rome at the Gregorian and at the Pontifical Oriental Institute, receiving a licentiate in theology and a doctorate in Canon Law. He is professor of Russian and of Canon Law at the Pontifical Oriental Institute. His published works include *A Study on the Chief Code of Russian Canon Law* (1964).

International Publishers of CONCILIUM

ENGLISH EDITION
Paulist Press
Paramus, N.J., U.S.A.

Burns & Oates Ltd.
25 Ashley Place
London, S.W.1

DUTCH EDITION
Uitgeverij Paul Brand, N.V.
Hilversum, Netherlands

FRENCH EDITION
Maison Mame
Tours/Paris, France

JAPANESE EDITION (PARTIAL)
Nansôsha
Tokyo, Japan

GERMAN EDITION
Verlagsanstalt Benziger & Co., A.G.
Einsiedeln, Switzerland

Matthias Grunewald-Verlag
Mainz, W. Germany

SPANISH EDITION
Ediciones Guadarrama
Madrid, Spain

PORTUGUESE EDITION
Livraria Morais Editora, Ltda.
Lisbon, Portugal

ITALIAN EDITION
Editrice Queriniana
Brescia, Italy

POLISH EDITION (PARTIAL)
Pallottinum
Poznan-Warsaw, Poland